shock and awe

war on words

Bregje van Eekelen
Jennifer González
Bettina Stötzer
Anna Tsing

editors

Feminisms and Global War Project
Institute for Advanced Feminist Research

new pacific press
Santa Cruz, California
2004

Published and distributed in the United States by
New Pacific Press
204 Locust Street
Santa Cruz, CA 95060

www.literaryguillotine.com/npp/npphome.html

First published 2004

10 9 8 7 6 5 4 3 2 1

New Pacific Press was established in 2003 as a "Hey, we'll at least break even" alternative to the commercial, homogeneous publications that currently dominate the publishing industry. New Pacific Press does not believe that it necessarily serves the public interest to operate a not-for-profit enterprise, but rather that there is both value and viability in publishing small, innovative, educational and culturally significant works that the mainstream may consider small potatoes. Our planned publications will be primarily sociopolitical, economic, cultural studies; they will be scholarly, personal, poetic, mixed-media presentations that reflect the multiplicity of cultural work being done in the greater Bay Area and throughout the Pacific Rim(s).

Cover design by Colleen Barclay

Book design by Stephen Pollard
Set in ITC American Typewriter and ITC Slimbach

Cover photo: Raging fire, Conservation Reserve Program (CRP) land, Lyon County, Kansas, by Larry Schwarm (courtesy of Robert Koch Gallery). If there is shock and awe, it is that the human spirit survives what others inflict.

ISBN 0-971-25460-5

Printed in Canada by Hemlock Printers Ltd.

contributors

Itty Abraham · Raymond Apthorpe · Dalit Baum
Amita Baviskar · Jonathan Beller · L. R. Berger
Iain Boal · Margaret Brose · Wendy Brown · Sean Burns
Wendy Call · Jeremy M. Campbell · Ben Carson
Kathryn Chetkovich · Martha Collins
Christopher Connery · Wendy Coxshall · Angela Y. Davis
Mike Davis · Hilla Dayan · Joseph Dumit · P. A. Ebron
Bregje van Eekelen · Lieba Faier · Kathy E. Ferguson
Courtney L. Fitzpatrick · Jonathan Fox · Carla Freccero
Carol Gluck · Myra Goldberg · Jennifer González
Lisbeth Haas · Donna Haraway · Sharon Hayes
Engseng Ho · Karen Z. Ho · Donna Hunter · Emily Jacir
NeEddra James · Sushma Joshi · Afsaneh Kalantary
S. Eben Kirksey · Morgen J. Lennox · Sven Lindqvist
Lydia H. Liu · Krista Geneviève Lynes · Bahíyyih Maroon
Julia Meltzer · Helene Moglen · Goenawan Mohamad
Annemarie Mol · Carole Simmons Oles · Geeta Patel
Mary Louise Pratt · Vicente L. Rafael · Lynn Randolph
Maple Razsa · Adrienne Rich · Lisa Rofel
Renato Rosaldo · AnnJanette Rosga · Martha Rosler
James K. Rowe · Warren Sack · Larry Schwarm
James C. Scott · Alix Kates Shulman · Bettina Stötzer
Marilyn Strathern · Neferti Tadiar · Kasian Tejapira
David Thorne · Jude Todd · Anna Tsing · Phyllis Turnbull
Yasushi Uchiyamada · Neerja Vasishta · Kath Weston

contents

war on words

Bregje van Eekelen

Jennifer González

Bettina Stötzer

Anna Tsing

Do words sometimes betray you, leaving you a stranger in your own land? Words can be brutal, frustrating, and exhausting. Consider terrorism, civilization, and even peace, family, and security. Words can also be bridges to new forms of experience and openings for alliance. This book explores the political trajectories of words through pictures, excerpts, stories and exegesis about the politics of the present global situation. Scholars, artists, activists and poets have joined forces to offer alternative etymologies, genealogies, fragments of everyday life, and glimpses of social history as a form of defense and defiance in an escalating war on words.

the president and the poet come to the negotiating table

L. R. Berger

I only agreed to compromise when it became clear
they were already stealing them again out from under us:
words, one at a time.

Okay, I said, like some ambassador for language
facing him hunched over my yellow pad of conditions.

He was wearing his orange tie and with the graciousness
of one who believes they have little to lose, he said,
There are far too many words, anyway.

Okay, then, I said, *you can have CONQUEST
and DOW JONES.
You can have BOMBS, but we want the SMART back.*

This was fine with him. He had plenty of other words
for SMART,
and would trade it for IMPERIAL and NUCLEAR.

TRADE is a word, I said, *you might as well keep,
but don't touch SHADOW or PHENOMENA.*

I gave up SOFT when paired with TARGETS
for the names of every bird. He said he'd consider
relinquishing CITIZEN for CUSTOMER.

I made my claim for CONSCIENCE, but he refused
until I sacrificed PERFECTION.

That's when he stood up shaking and wagging
    his finger at me.
He had spotted GOD upside-down on my list.

Under no circumstances, he said, *do you get GOD,*
and only calmed down when he heard me announce
I completely agreed with him.

GOD, I said, *must be returned to God.*

But this wasn't what he had in mind.
In his mind were SHOCK and AWE.

SHOCK was the word to bring me to my feet,
because poets can rise up angry and shaking
for what they love too.

SHOCK, I said. *You can have SHOCK.*
But AWE—over my dead body.

Reprinted from *Peacework* with author's permission

accident

see **weapons of mass destruction**

airport

Renato Rosaldo

Uniforms strut with dogs,
find a fingernail clipper,

command, *Spread your legs,*
hands up, unbuckle

that belt, let it drop.
Now my shoes provoke

security designed to make me
bow down, tolerate any invasion.

aliens

Amita Baviskar

alien 4. of a nature different from. This passes imperceptibly
into: **5.** repugnant and unwelcome; **6.** unkindly and cold
—Oxford English Dictionary

In order to safeguard national security, the U.S. government has sharpened its scrutiny of aliens. Aliens are
now deemed the enemy within U.S. borders, a potential
threat to American citizens. The categories "citizen" and
"alien" appear to be clear-cut and counterposed: there
are citizens and there are aliens, legal and illegal. Legal aliens have been officially allowed to enter the U.S.
Let in by ostensibly liberal immigration policies, they

have contended with the inbuilt racism of country quotas—different rules for Nigerians and Norwegians—at embassies across the world. They have been fingerprinted and photographed, their family-financial-medical-criminal-political history—their personal effects—have become the property of the U.S. government. Invasive cross-examinations, pinprick insults and indignities are the price they have paid to live, for a limited period, in the land of the free.

Illegal aliens have had a harder time. Hunted in Texas by heat-seeking spotting scopes, now wielded by gun-toting private militias in combat fatigues, they have stolen across the border in search of a better life, taking on backbreaking tasks for less than minimum wage. Officially decried, their presence is tolerated and even actively encouraged in some quarters. These are the strawberry pickers and construction workers, baby-sitters and house cleaners, whose vulnerability is easy to exploit. This is the risk they take; if they can get in and stay below the radar, they may some day become legal. There are aliens who hope to accelerate amnesty and become legal American residents. They have enlisted in the U.S. Army in Iraq, fighting a war that isn't theirs, for a Green Card that may well be awarded post-humously. They join the ranks of a long line of reluctant recruits, slaves and subject races conscripted into foreign wars—the buffalo soldiers immortalized by Bob Marley, "stolen from Africa," and fighting Native Americans; and Indian peasants who died in the freezing mud of WW I trenches in Belgium—fighting for empire and their place in the sun.

At different times, the alien/citizen boundary has been policed with varying degrees of diligence. Well-behaved aliens have been offered hope, the possibility of a happy ending, if they become American. Like alien species, they can naturalize. People and plants from elsewhere can assimilate and adapt. Eucalypts and aca-cias, Central Americans and Chinese, they can all put down roots and flourish in foreign environs. But there are many who find this hybrid vigor alarming. Purists protest that native species are endangered and jobs threatened. Alien invasions—the fear of being overrun —is the stuff of science fiction. The horror films of the Cold War years depicted organized attacks by "social" animals, mirroring and magnifying anxieties about Red Army cadres marching across America. The notion of an American nature and culture at risk continues to haunt contemporary politics. The desire for racial and ecological purity lurks even among members of liberal environmental organizations like the Sierra Club, for whom ecological conservation entails stemming the tide of immigration.

The fear of the alien in our midst comes to the fore in times of crisis, when even citizens become suspect. 9/11 was one such moment. You may be a citizen born and bred, and still be regarded as alien. Your name, features and physiognomy, cast of eye and color of skin, mark you as "other." Japanese-Americans, Mexican-Americans, Arab-Americans—hyphenated identities raise questions. Where does your allegiance lie? In times of trouble, will you be loyal to your nation? If there is a doubt, your own government, the guarantor of your freedoms, may intern you or secretly monitor your life. You can be declared an enemy combatant and tortured in Guantánamo Bay, without recourse to the Geneva Conventions or your own Constitution, denied human rights and civil liberties. Your fellow-citizens can turn against you. You, more than anyone else, have to fly a flag, prove that you're a patriot. You may be a citizen but still never belong, for a part of you will always be marked: alien. As citizens, the alien is not only amidst you; the alien is inside you.

alone

see **beard**

America
from Nagano

Lieba Faier

"Lieba-*san's* lifestyle . . . in America . . . *sugoku ii deshô. Urayamashii, watashi wa* (. . . it's really good, isn't it? I'm jealous)," my Filipina friend Marivic sidestepped my question in her usual mixture of English and Japanese. We were sitting in the tidy three-room apartment she shared with her Japanese husband and children in the government-subsidized apartment complex on the Kiso River. I had asked Marivic about her childhood in the Philippines and why she had initially come to Japan as an "entertainer." She was embarrassed to tell me, she had demurred, and she had redirected the conversation back to America, where I gathered she had been heading all along. "New York?" she posed assuredly. "Los Angeles," I responded. Her eyes floated into the distance, "*My* grandfather's *older brother went into the* U.S. Navy *and so now they're in the* U.S., *in* Los Angeles. *They're doing* nursing. Is it easy to go now if you're a nurse in the Philippines? If you pass a test?"

During the nearly two years I lived in rural Nagano, most Filipina migrants I met were more eager to talk to me about America than just about anything else. Their questions were portals to a cosmopolitan world, a world full of glamour, wealth, beauty, and excitement. The majority of these women had traveled to Japan for "a better life," one they found working in Filipina hostess bars and in marriages with Japanese men. But their desires had been focused on another place: "America." Japan was just a way station on the road to their dreams. And just as "America" had given form to these women's desires, it had materially shaped the kinds of futures that they could imagine. In the mid-1970s, the U.S.-backed Marcos regime encouraged overseas labor migration as a national development strategy to bring much needed foreign currency into the collapsing Philippine economy. Also during the 1970s, the U.S. military began to bring Filipinas to entertain soldiers around U.S. bases in Okinawa. Soon, "structural adjustment" policies meant that many Filipinos/as had little choice but to look for employment in other parts of the world. By the mid-1980s, there were Filipina hostess bars throughout Japan, even in the remote mountains of rural Nagano.

Conversations about "America" I had with Filipina migrants in Japan always hinged on the privileges of my global status, just as our discussions rested on the constraints and vulnerabilities of theirs. Women told me with pride and longing about sisters, cousins, aunts, and uncles who lived in New Jersey, Oregon, Arkansas, and even Canada. They spoke of longstanding desires to visit the United States, asking if one could become eligible for a tourist visa if she became a permanent resident of Japan or a Japanese national. Consistently when I met a Filipina migrant in Japan, the first question she asked was: "What kind of visa do you have and how did you get it?" A woman named Susie to whom I was introduced at a party asked me straight away if it were easy to get a visa as an "American." She had just arrived in Japan on a spousal visa, her recent marriage arranged through a cousin also wed to a Japanese man. *Only rich people in the Philippines can get tourist visas,* she told me in Tagalog as she turned her eyes away from mine.

If these Filipino women had taken desires for "America" with them when they had gone to Japan, they amalgamated these dreams with the possibilities they found in rural Nagano. Their lives as bar hostesses and as wives and mothers there were part of that alchemy of coercion and desire through which America is made all over the globe. Through my relationships with these women, I came to see America as both a brutal political economic force and a metaphor for dreams, as a figure of the interconnected and intersecting desires and realities that had unequally brought us all to Japan. And as Filipino women I met invoked America in such terms, they taught me to see it in new and different ways. They showed me that America was not that solitary home that the U.S. government tells us is always in danger of being destroyed. It was also that small place, full of pain and promise, that these women were configuring through their lives in rural Nagano.

America
from Abu Ghraib

Wendy Brown

The torture and abuse perpetrated by American troops at the Abu Ghraib prison in Iraq raises a panoply of questions: Who ordered or condoned it? Who knew what, when? Who will be brought to account and who should be brought to account? Who thought up the particulars of the abuse? What was its aim or purpose? How systematic were these purposes? How much of what happened was simply sport for bored prison guards? In what ways does the pornographic racism, misogyny and homophobia of the torture mirror American culture, or military culture, or Western culture? How does the abuse at Abu Ghraib link with abuse of prisoners in American prisons, and with the American imaginary about all of its "others"?

These are important questions for Americans coming to terms with the sources and dynamics of an imperial mentality menacing both the world and what remains of the integrity of the United States. But these questions are also all about us . . . again. They are questions for us, the perpetrators, through which we try to understand ourselves. They do not query the story Abu Ghraib tells *about us* to the targets or those who identify with the targets of American imperial aggression.

What does America look like to the world in these pictures?

Bullying and decadent, glorying in inherited power and wealth. The images from Abu Ghraib do not depict systematic efforts at producing war intelligence or disciplining prisoners but the frat-party prankster profligacy of the arrogant and entitled on a drunken spree. Yet the images of the power of an aggressive regime disseminated to its lower classes are also frighteningly reminiscent of Nazi Gestapo youth in the early days of the Third Reich, licensed to vent their class resentments as thuggish brutality and sadistic humiliation on state-designated targets.

Depraved. However one reads the complex pornography of hatred in the staged tableaux as well as the reports of routine sodomy, rape, necrophilia, and general sexual humiliation of Abu Ghraib prisoners, it screams depravity. Whether figuring Iraqi women, men and children as animals, or as objects of sexual sadism, humiliation, brutality or ridicule, the scenes suggest no bottom and no outside edge to this depravity, no limits defined either by moral or human decency.

Stupid, Profligate, Indulgent. The aimless bullying and the sexual entertainment that the torture of the prisoners appeared to provide, combined with the idiotically grinning faces of the American GIs presiding over the scenes of abuse, together carry an image of America as glutted, aimless and juvenile in its absorptions and pleasures. Many of the images convey scenes of such a superfluity of power that there is no way to spend it other than on foolish pranks, pointless cruelties, idle humiliations. Boys pulling wings off flies on a long summer day.

Sex-obsessed. The images of those tortured to death are deeply disturbing. Yet they are swamped and diminished by the pileup of images of sexual humiliation and abuse. The sheer quantity and variety of the sexual scenes suggest that there is nothing with which Americans are more preoccupied, except perhaps access to Middle Eastern oil.

Supremacist, Disdainful and Contemptuous. The scenes and stories of torture convey not simply hatred but disdain and contempt for Arabs and Muslims, for other cultures, other ways of living and believing. We are human; they are animal, worthy neither of being known in their complexity or respected in the essential dignity that the International Declaration of Human Rights asserts for all humans. This contempt is complexly circuited through America's own local hatreds and contempt, its homophobia, misogyny and racisms. Thus, the prisoners' forced consumption of alcohol, forced denunciations of Islam, forced nudity, forced homosexual acts and forced exposure to bare-breasted women produce a reverberation between internal American hatreds and contempt for the cultural other. The acts mobilized the hatreds that swirl beneath American professions of equality, secularism, civility, and tolerance and poured them into the essence of the not-American. In the pornography of militarized hatreds, Muslims, brown-skinned people, Arabic speakers, women, and homosexuals are all merged into scenes in which the one is made to stand in for, even morph into, the other.[1]

· · ·

Abu Ghraib confirmed an image of America much of the world already saw in the launching of the Iraq war, an act that spurned internationalism, truth, knowledge, and political foresight, and deployed superpower for purposes of raw domination and personal glory. The prism of Abu Ghraib confirms a perception of America as a gluttonous bully, vile and violent, stupid and bellicose, projecting its depravity, ignorance, and monstrousness onto others as it screeches moral righteousness believed by no one but its own.

There is this America today, profoundly corrupted by its twentieth-century accumulation of power and wealth untempered by thinking, responsibility, and humility. There is this America in which "democracy" stands for little more than decadent indulgences, ignorant supremacism, and imperial designs. There is this America driven only by the raw passion of "I want" and the raw fact of "I can!" This America has rightly made G. W. Bush its president for they mirror each other.

But there are yet and still other Americas, which we will fail to bring forth at the world's peril, and our own.

---

[1]A recently leaked U.S. government survey of Iraqi political views indicated that 71 percent of Iraqis were surprised by the torture at Abu Ghraib, and of these, 48 percent were surprised because the torture "humiliated Iraqis." The abuse, then, illuminated a level of contempt for Iraqis that most of the population, even in its cynicism about American war aims, was not prepared for. However, the survey also indicated that 54 percent of Iraqis believe that all Americans behave as the GIs at Abu Ghraib did. "Public Opin-

ion in Iraq," June 15, 2004 (www.msnbc.msn.com/id/5217741/
site/newsweek). Although they surveyed less than 2000 random
Iraqis in 5 cities, there is a lot in the poll that is fascinating,
including the fact that a sobering 2 percent of Iraqis consider
Americans "liberators" while over 90 percent consider them
"occupiers."

anarchism

Wendy Call

The night before we left for Iran, the police came to visit us. At home. (They never asked us about our travel
plans and we never mentioned them.) The state trooper
had told us on the phone he was coming over because,
"We have some property that we believe belongs to
you." In the end, that was partly true. They returned a
computer that had been stolen—along with many other
things—from our car. Eighteen months earlier.

Two men walked into our house that evening. One
held up my long-missing laptop bag and said, "Does
this look familiar?"

They sat in our dining room for nearly an hour,
questioning us—not about the robbery, but about some
of the files they had found on our computer. "Lots of
stuff about anarchism," one of them said—the one from
the "Special Investigations Unit." They told us they had
found the documents when they removed the laptop's
hard disk and handed it over to their Forensics Unit.

We tried to tell them about the other things that had
been stolen from our car—especially about the check-
book later used to spend thousands of dollars at Wal-
Mart and Family Dollar.

Before the state trooper and the Special Investiga-
tor showed up, I had spent most of that day reassuring friends and family who called to wish us well in

Iran. No, I wasn't scared to go there. Yes, I was excited about meeting my partner's father for the first time. No, I didn't expect there to be any problems. As I discovered that evening at our dining room table, the problems would occur before we left. Why couldn't we read or write about anarchism—about self-determination and political freedom and responsibility—without the Special Investigations Unit showing up at our home? The Democratic National Convention was coming to our city in a few months, the two men explained. "We're checking stuff like this out."

They wanted to root out any potential violence.

anti-terror legislation

Bettina Stötzer

U.S. "anti-terror" and "security" measures have found their counterparts across Europe. While U.S. Americans and Europeans have not always seen eye to eye on imperial aggression, the power of U.S. policy has been to reproduce its categories even in European countries where they are popularly opposed. Consider the parallelism among the following pieces of anti-terror legislation, each passed after the events of September 11, 2001.[1]

USA PATRIOT Act (October 2001, U.S.): According to the U.S. government website, the purpose of this Act is to protect "the homeland, enabling the Federal government to better track terrorists, disrupt their cells, and seize their assets. By breaking down unnecessary barriers between intelligence and law enforcement officers, the PATRIOT Act is helping to ensure that the best available information about terrorist threats is provided to the people who need it most" (www.whitehouse.gov/homeland). The PATRIOT Act has expanded observance of the movements of suspicious "foreign nationals" and the surveillance of phone and Internet communication. It has allowed indefinite detention of "suspicious subjects" without cause. The Department of Homeland Security has planned an extensive surveillance system for the collection of biometric data on people visiting the U.S.

Anti-Terrorism, Crime and Security Act 2001 (ATCSA, December 2001, U.K.): The ATCSA authorized the police to conduct passport controls, searches and arrests during protests; it introduced restrictions to the rights of prisoners to seek legal advice, the right to the presumption of innocence, the right to a defense and the right to counsel; it allowed non-U.K. nationals to be detained potentially indefinitely if suspected of international "terrorist activity."

Loi d'orientation et de programmation pour la sécurité interieure (LOPSI, "Internal Security Law," November 2001/August 2002, France): LOPSI expanded the powers of the police and relaxed the requirements to justify searches and to retain computerized personal data about "suspect" persons; it targeted specific social groups such as homeless people, sex workers, and "illegal immigrants" and introduced stricter punishments—including imprisonment and large fines—for gatherings in public spaces within residential apartment blocks, public soliciting, "aggressive" collective begging, swearing at or insulting public officials, and insulting the national flag and national anthem at certain public events.

Terrorismusbekämpfungsgesetz ("Law to Combat Terrorism," also referred to as *"Anti-Terror-Paket,"* "Anti-Terror-Package," December 2001, Germany): The *Terrorismusbekämpfungsgesetz* encompasses about a hundred legal changes, ranging from the permission to include biometric data in passports, the introduction of more extensive video surveillance in public spaces, reforms in asylum and immigration law, to the expansion of the state's rights to gather personal data, especially on foreign students and employees in the realm of public health, media and energy production.

---

[1]Amnesty International, Annual Report 2004 (web.amnesty.org/report2004/index-eng); "Republik der Flics" *Jungle World* 43 (October 16, 2002); "Das Anti-Terror-Monstrum" *Spiegel,* November 26, 2002 (www.spiegel.de/politik/ausland/0,1518,224358,00.html).

barbarian

Lydia H. Liu

In 1858 the Sino-British Treaty of Tianjin made it illegal to offer any but one translation for the Chinese word "yi." From this point onwards, "yi" would mean "barbarian" and nothing else. The English hoped to straighten the matter out, to settle once and for all the barbarity of Chinese classification.

The rhetoric of civilization and barbarity has made a comeback. We are told that the clash of civilizations is what has caused global military conflicts. We hear that Western civilization is poised once again to conquer barbarity. When it comes to colonial warfare, some things never go away.

One of the least understood aspects of the Opium Wars in the nineteenth century is precisely how the British opium dealers sold the war to Parliament and the British public. The rhetoric of civilization and barbarity was central to their claims. But the familiar rhetoric underwent a most bizarre twist: Even as the British spoke of the Chinese as "barbarians," they were nonetheless troubled by the thought that the Chinese might be regarding them in a reciprocal manner. The evidence of disrespect thus became a focal point in early Anglo-Chinese diplomatic disputes as the British repeatedly sought reparations for the damages done to their national honor. The war on the barbaric treatment of the Englishmen as "barbarians" by the Chinese evolved into a major episode during the early military confrontation that culminated in the first Opium War in 1839. Thus arose the popular ethnocentric view in the West that the Chinese invariably look down upon outsiders as barbarians.

Article 51 of the Sino-British Treaty of Tianjin stipulated in 1858 that "It is agreed, that henceforward the character 夷 ('barbarian') shall not be applied to the Government or subjects of Her Britannic Majesty, in any Chinese official document issued by the Chinese Authorities, either in the Capital or in the Provinces." The prohibited written Chinese character (read *yi* in modern Pinyin romanization) had been routinely applied to foreigners by the Qing government. On the Chinese side, it was determined that this character meant "foreigner" but the British authorities insisted that this word should be translated as "barbarian" and inserted the same in the treaty text. On the basis of that translation, the British charged that the Chinese mistreated the British and Europeans as "barbarians" and sought to ban the word *yi* for good. The character has since disappeared from the vocabulary of the living Chinese language.

In what ways does the Chinese written character pose a threat to law and to the emergent order of international relations? The British East India Company in China had always translated the character *yi* as "foreigner" in the eighteenth century and through the first three decades of the nineteenth century. This interpretation was endorsed by the British missionary

Robert Morrison, who glossed *yi* and *yi ren* as "foreigner" in his *English Dictionary of the Chinese Language* (1815–1820), the first of its kind. From 1834 onwards, the British government began to take over the task of translation and manage the flow of diplomatic correspondences with the Qing government. It was in his capacity as the official interpreter of Lord Napier that Robert Morrison recanted his earlier decision and began to translate the character *yi* as "barbarian." The strategic revision played right into the confrontational strategy adopted by Lord Palmerston, Lord Napier, and opium dealers in China.

The first military clash between the British navy and the Qing troops was occasioned not by the opium trade but by the alleged Chinese disrespectful treatment of Lord Napier as *yimu* (Chief Superintendent of British Trade), a word understood by the British as meaning "Barbarian Eye." In the parliamentary debates that ensued, the Chinese insult of foreigners was cited as an act of moral injury, which justified the demand for reparations and military assault. When Queen Victoria gave her speech to Parliament on January 26, 1841 at the close of the first Opium War, she stated: "Having deemed it necessary to send to the coast of China a naval and military force, to demand reparation and redress for the injuries inflicted upon some of my subjects by the officers of the Emperor of China, and for indignities offered to an Agent of my Crown, I, at the same time, appointed Plenipotentiaries to treat upon these matters with the Chinese Government." The injuries and indignities to which the queen referred include not only the seizure of illicit British opium by the Chinese government but also certain disrespectful words such as the character *yi*.

In the U.S. war on terrorism, the idea of a "preemptive strike" presupposes the threat of injury by the barbaric other, although WMD in Iraq is as much a figment of the imperial imagination as was the Chinese injury of British honor more than a century ago. It is not by accident that the shareholders of some of the major multinational oil companies doing business in the Middle East happen to be the direct heirs of the British opium dealers in the Far East.

beard, shave, dental, hair, alone

Krista Geneviève Lynes

These titles, the tenuous start of a wartime haiku, name the images in the CNN photo essay of Saddam Hussein's capture. What can be gleaned from these video stills? What argument might they propose? The visual toolbox opens and a few devices, tricks of the trade, shortcuts and rhetorical flourishes pop out.

The essay proceeds in pairs and ends with a single image, actually entitled "Alone," whose pair we have to imagine. The first two images in the series—"Beard" and "Shave"—set up a narrative of revelation. Saddam Hussein is captured (on film) and exposed. The black bars on either side of the image and Saddam Hussein's front and three-quarter view locate Hussein as a "criminal type." We are already in thick image histories: Alphonse Bertillon's early photographs of criminals, Charcot's hysterics at the Salpetrière, O. J. Simpson on the covers of *Time* and *Newsweek*. If these photos look like mug shots, it is because Hussein is already indicted.

The next two images are linked formally by their fluorescent hue, as well as by the military doctor who figures in both shots as an inspector. These are video stills from the Coalition Provisional Authority, little congealed moments of an overall fastidious inspec-

tion. Entitled "Dental" and "Hair," the images fragment Saddam Hussein's body into specimens. Hussein is photographed against a tile background, evoking a sense of the clinical nature of the inspection, particularly in the light of the antiseptic touch of the doctor—his rubber gloves, his tongue depressor, his bald clean head. Even his glasses shield his eyes from Hussein's "messy" body. The tile background not only evokes a bathroom-cum-doctor's office, scientific lab, or torture chamber; it is also a grid against which Saddam Hussein is measured (up). Like early scientific and ethnographic photographs, which sought to map racial or sexual hierarchies onto unsuspecting body parts, these photographs not only show an unruly body inspected by the clinical hand of science, but also the measurement of Saddam Hussein against an anthropometric ruler: he becomes transformed into a racial type, as if by magic.

The final image is enigmatic: not paired with another photograph, ending actually with Hussein prior to his inspection and shave, this singular image, "Alone," concludes the essay. Hussein is now a wayward son, banished from the "Family of Man" (the iconic banner of the "Coalition of the Willing"). The maps behind his head can be literalized: he is alone in the world, except of course for the Coalition Provisional Authority photographer, recording his troubled gaze, and of course for our look upon him. We are not keeping good company with him. The essay ends not with Saddam Hussein revealed (we have been treated to that up front, as if impatient to see with our own eyes), but with an anxious Hussein, not ready for the inspection we already know he will undergo. He is not only alone, but also unknowing. We, on the other hand, know what will happen to him. After months of frenzied media anxiety about Saddam Hussein's whereabouts, we are no longer uncertain of his future (a barely veiled threat), but he is.

black feminist warrior poets

Bahíyyih Maroon

An ever-expanding collective of writers dedicated to claiming a place in the world as none other than their essential free selves. First coined by the late Audre Lorde, who authored *Zami: A New Spelling of My Name* and *The Marvelous Arithmetics of Distance,* among numerous other works, the phrase has come to signify a way of declaring resistance, activism and liberatory modes of existing in the world—even when this world is hostile to the fact of the body in question. Posthumously inaugurated members of this collective include Bessie Smith, Zora Neale Hurston, Sojourner Truth and Fannie Lou Hamer. Among the collective's influential members are June Jordan, who walked in life on stars and made even hardened anger into a sustaining molasses to savor; Sonia Sanchez, who rebirthed the haiku into a literary jazz form for free thought; and the illustrious Hattie Gossett, whose writings on the black body inspire joyous laughter, comforting recognition and illuminated inroads of self-respect. More recent additions are the novelist poet Sapphire, who has brought language to those silenced by illiteracy's tyrannies; Ruth Foreman, whose words conjure the improbable as sweet morning tides of infinite hope; and Safiya Henderson Holmes, who once declared that the most beautiful kitchen in the world is made of sunrise orange tiles and best enjoyed without the percolations of sorrow's worn pots. Opening boundaries and honoring ancestors in the same turn, younger members of the collective include "sounded language" artist Latasha Natasha Diggs; queer hip-hop memoirist Tim'm West; and Lisa Moore, whose publishing company RedBone Press stands alongside Kitchen Table Press as a vital and vibrant vehicle for promoting prolific declarations of being in language, love, and liberation as emancipatory principles of everyday life.

the bombs

Martha Collins

We hit the train we are sorry it was a mistake.
We hit those refugees sorry another mistake.
We hit the bridge there were people we couldn't see.
We hit the water supply not a mistake but we are sorry.

We hit the embassy sorry another mistake.
We hit the wrong country it wasn't planned.
In the past we have also hit the wrong things
    a passenger plane a school.
This time the reasons for hitting what we were trying
    to hit were good.
We were trying to stop the terrible things being done
    to innocent people.
Things got worse for those people after we started
    which proves we were right.
But of course we cannot think about what is right
    or what is wrong.
They call us smart but bombs are not made to think.
We are sorry there were mistakes but we ourselves
    make no mistakes.
We only follow orders. We do what we're told.

First published in *Witness*

chicken

Donna Haraway

Chicken is no coward. Indeed, this warrior bird has plied his trade as a fighting cock around the world since the earliest days such fowl consented to work for people, somewhere in south and southeast Asia.

Anxious if brave, Chicken Little has long worried that the sky is falling. He has a good vantage point from which to assess this matter; for Chicken, right along with his overreaching companion, *Homo sapiens,* has been witness and participant in all the big events of Civilization. Chicken labored on the Egyptian pyramids, when barley-pinching Pharaohs got the world's first mass egg industry going to feed the avians' co-conscripted human workers. Much later—a bit after the Egyptians replaced their barley exchange system with proper coins, thus acting like the progressive capitalists their exchange partners always seem to want in that part of the world— Julius Caesar brought the Pax Romana, along with the "ancient English" chicken breed, the Dorking, to Britain. Chicken Little knows all about the shock and awe of History, and he is a master at tracking the routes of Globalizations, old and new. Technoscience is no stranger either. Add to that, Chicken knows a lot about Biodiversity and Cultural Diversity, whether one thinks about the startling variety of chicken-kind for the 5000 years of their domestic arrangements with humanity, or considers the "improved breeds" accompanying capitalist class formations from the nineteenth century to now. No county fair is complete without its gorgeous "purebred" chickens, who know a lot about the history of eugenics. It is hard to sort out shock from awe in chicken-land. Whether the firmament takes a calamitous tumble or not, Chicken holds up a good half of the sky.

In 2004 C.E., Chicken Little donned his spurs once more and entered the war on words thrust on him by Current Events. Ever a gender bender, Chicken joined the GLBT Brigade and outdid himself as a postcolonial, transnational, pissed-off spent hen and mad feminist. Chicken admitted that s/he was inspired by the all (human) girl underground fight clubs that s/he found out about on www.extremechickfights.com. Ignoring the sexism of "chick"—extreme or not—and the porn industry and pedophilic scene that vilifies the name of chicken, our Bird raptured those fighting girls right out of History and into his trannie sf world, fit to confront the Eagles of War and the Captains of Industry. S/he felt this rapturous power because s/he recalled not just the exploits of Cousin Phoenix, but also the years when s/he was a figure of Jesus Resurrected, promising the faithful that they would rise from the ashes of History's barbecues.

Barbecue. An unkind reminder of where Chicken Little had best concentrate her attention. For, at the end of a millennium, in 2000, 10 billion chickens were slaughtered in the U.S. alone. Worldwide, 5 billion hens—75 percent in cramped, multi-occupancy quarters called battery cages—were laying eggs, with Chinese flocks leading the way, followed by those in the United States and Europe. Thai chicken exports topped $1.5 billion in value in an industry supplying Japanese and E.U. markets and employing hundreds of thousands of Thai citizens. World chicken production was 65.6 million tons, and the whole operation was growing at 4 percent per year. Captains of Industry, indeed. Chicken could conclude that her/his major vocation seems to be breakfast and dinner while the world burns.[1]

Contrary to the views of her pesky friends in the transnational animal rights movement, our Opportunistic Bird is not against surrendering a pound of flesh in exchange for pecking rights in the naturalcultural contractual arrangements that domesticated both bipedal hominids and winged gallinaceous avians. But there's something seriously foul in current versions of multispecies global contract theory.

One way to tell the trouble—one detail among myriads—is that a three-year study in Tulsa, Oklahoma—a center of factory chicken production—showed that half the water supply was dangerously polluted by poultry waste. Go ahead, microwave sponges in your kitchens as often as the clean food cops advise; inventive bacteria will outwit you with their fowl alliances.

Well, one more detail. Manipulated genetically since the 1950s to rapidly grow mega breasts, chickens, given a choice, choose food laced with pain killers. "Unsustainable growth rates" are supposed to be about dot-com fantasies and inflationary stock markets. In Chicken's world, however, that term designates the daily immolation of forced maturation and disproportionate tissue development that produces tasty (enough) young birds unable to walk, flap their wings, or even stand up. Muscles linked in evolutionary history and religious symbolism to flight, sexual display, and transcendence instead pump iron for transnational growth industries. Not satisfied, some agribusiness scientists look to post-genomics research for even more buffed white meat.[2]

The first farm animals to be permanently confined indoors and made to labor in automated systems based on Technoscience's finest genetic technologies, feed-conversion efficiency research, and miracle drugs (not pain killers, but antibiotics and hormones), Chicken might be excused for being unimpressed by the McDonald's Corporation's grudging agreement in 2000 to require that its suppliers give 50 percent more space per bird destined to be Chicken McNuggets and Eggs McMuffin. Still, McDonald's was the first corporation in the world to admit that pain and suffering are concepts familiar to underrated bird brains. Chicken's ingratitude is no wonder, when no humane slaughter law in the U.S. or Canada to this day applies to chickens.

In 1999 the E.U. did manage to ban battery cages—beginning in 2012. That should allow for a smooth transition. Perhaps more sensitized to ever-ready holocaust analogies, the Germans will make those cages illegal in 2007. In the market-besotted U.S., Chicken's hope seems to be in designer eggs for the omega-3 fatty acid–conscious and free-range certified organic chickens for the conscience-stricken and pure of diet. The up-to-the-minute ethically fastidious might procure their chicken fix like the citizens in Margaret Atwood's sf novel *Oryx and Crake* (2003). There, chicken knobs—tasty organs without organisms, especially without annoying heads that register pain and perhaps have ideas about what constitutes a proper domestic bird's life—are on the menu. Genetically engineered muscles-without-animals illustrate exactly what Sarah Franklin means by designer ethics, which aim to bypass cultural struggle with just-in-time, "high technology" breakthroughs.[3] Design away the controversy, and all those free-range anarchists will have to go home. But remember, Chicken squawks even when his head has been cut off.

The law cannot be counted on. After all, even human laborers in the chicken industry are super-exploited. Thinking of battery cages for laying hens reminds Chicken Little how many illegal immigrants, un-unionized women and men, people of color, and former prisoners process chickens in Georgia, Arkansas, and Ohio. It's no wonder that at least one U.S. soldier who tortured Iraqi prisoners was a chicken processor in her civilian life.

Sick

It's enough to make a sensitive Bird sick, as much from the virus of transnational politics as from the other kind. An avian flu outbreak in seven Asian nations shocked the world in the last four months of 2003. Luckily, only a few humans died, unlike the tens of millions who succumbed in 1918–19. But before the 2004 fears abated, about 20 million chickens were prophylactically slaughtered in Thailand alone. Global TV news showed unprotected human workers stuffing innumerable birds into sacks, tossing them undead into mass graves, and sprinkling on lime. In Thailand, 99 percent of chicken operations are, in Globalspeak, "small" (fewer than 1000 birds, since it takes more than 80,000 to be "large") and could not afford biosecurity—for people or birds. Newscasters waxed eloquent about a threatened transnational industry, but spoke nary a word about farmers' and chickens' lives. Meanwhile, Indonesian government spokespeople in

2003 denied any avian flu in those salubrious quarters, even while Indonesian veterinary associations argued that millions of birds showed signs of avian flu as early as October.

Perhaps the Bangkok *Post* on January 27, 2004 got the war of worlds, words, and images right, with a cartoon showing migratory birds from the north dropping bombs—bird shit full of avian flu strain H5N1—on the geobody of the Thai nation.

This postcolonial joke on trans-border bioterrorism is a nice reversal of U.S. and European fears of immigrants of all species from the global south. After all, prototypes for technoscientific, export-oriented, epidemic-friendly chicken industries were big on the Peace Corps agenda (a theme picked up later by GATT), right along with artificial milk for infants. Proud progenitor of such meaty progress, the U.S. had high hopes for winning the Cold War in Asia with standardized broilers and layers carrying democratic values. In Eugene Burdick and William J. Lederer's 1958 novel *The Ugly American,* set in a fictional southeast Asian nation called Sarkan, Iowa chicken farmer and agricultural teacher Tom Knox was about the only decent U.S. guy. Neither Knox nor subsequent Development Experts seem to have cared much for the varied chicken-human livelihoods thriving for a long time throughout Asia.

Chicken Little is, of course, no virgin to debates about political orders. The darling of savants' disputes about the nature of mind and instincts, the "philosopher's chick" was a staple of nineteenth-century learned idioms. Famous experiments in comparative psychology gave the world the term "pecking order" in the 1920s. Chicken Little remembers that this research by the Norwegian Thorleif Schjelderup-Ebbe, a serious lover and student of chickens, described complex social arrangements worthy of fowl, not the wooden dominance hierarchies in biopolitics that gained such a hold on cultural imaginations. Behavioral sciences of both human and non-human varieties continue to find anything but dominance and subordination hard to think about. Chicken knows that getting better accounts of animal doings, with each other and with humans, can play an important role in reclaiming livable politics.

Laying hens and fertile eggs dominate Chicken Little's closing thoughts. Perversely, s/he finds there the stuff of freedom projects and renewed awe. The British animation film *Chicken Run* (2000) stars 1950s Yorkshire hens facing a life of forced toil. The appearance of Rocky, the Rhode Island Red, catalyzes a liberation drama that gives no comfort either to "deep animal rights" imaginations of a time before co-species domestication nor to millennial free traders in chicken flesh. Pecking hens have other biopolitical tricks tucked under their wings.

Chicken Little returns in the end to the egg—fertile eggs in school biology labs that once gave millions of young hominids the privilege to see the shocking beauty of the developing chick embryo, with its dynamic architectural intricacies. These cracked-open eggs did not offer an innocent beauty, but they also gave no warrant to colonial or postcolonial arrogances about Development. They can renew the meaning of awe in a world in which laying hens know more about the alliances it will take to survive and flourish in multi-species, multi-cultural, multi-ordered associations than do all the secondary Bushes in Florida and Washington. Follow the chicken and find the world.

The sky has not fallen, not yet.

---

[1]Figures are from United Poultry Concerns, online.

[2]Myostatin regulates muscle development, and its gene is under intense scrutiny. Commercial interest relates to the world's number one genetic disease (muscular dystrophies), wasting

disorders (including aging and AIDS-related muscle loss), space flight–induced muscle atrophy, sports (watch out, steroid purveyors!), and bigger chicken muscles.

[3]Sarah Franklin, "Stem Cells R Us," in A. Ong and S. Collier, eds., *Global Assemblages* (London: Blackwell, 2004), 59–78.

civilization

Anna Tsing

Professor Samuel P. Huntington has argued that the world today is best characterized as a "clash of civilizations." U.S. foreign policy had worked hard to produce just this effect. The following diagram is adapted from Huntington's 1996 book.[1]

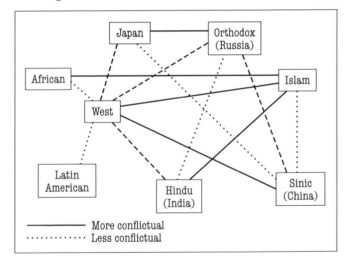

To read this diagram, you must agree that:

1 Despite migration, conquest, and cultural change, the world is divided into discrete self-governing civilizations.

2 The West has shifted to the "western" side of the map as the United States has assumed unquestioned leadership of the world's Christian peoples.

3 The major threat to Western hegemony is found in the East.

4 "Islam" and "China," the two great civilizations of the East, are allied against the West.

5 Eastern orthodox Christianity defines the political culture of post-communist Russia—making it a potential Western ally. Muslim Russians must therefore be foreign subversives.

6 Africans are never Muslims.

7 Latin America is the most isolated place in the world, maintaining ties only with the U.S.-led "West."

Which of these statements are true?

---

[1]Samuel P. Huntington, *The Clash of Civilizations and the Remaking of World Order* (New York: Simon and Schuster, 1996), 245.

coalition
a device

Carole Simmons Oles

coalition
coal it ion ton on tan ali con tic clit lit loon lot not nit
tin loin tao nil coat loci lint loan toil colt tonal coot
cool tool loot coon a an clan can talc act action in on

"Coalition" aircraft have bombed Baghdad again.
Two-thousand-pound bombs lit the night sky,
fires leaving a talc over hair and bare loins.
A rival clan will loot the city. Why not?

Tin merchants' shops the loci of precision
action gone wrong. Survivors toil
through the lot for a chunk of coal,
a can of beans. Ali calls like a loon
to his son. Nil. Not even a coat.
Just an ion in the tonal silence.

Tao for the people:
    Bombs are failure's tool, "liberation" its con.
    You are the coalition. Act.

collaborations

Adrienne Rich

I

Thought of this "our" nation :: thought of war
                              ghosts of war fugitive
    in labyrinths of amnesia
veterans   out-of-date textbooks in a library basement
evidence trundled off   plutonium   under traps after
    dark
            didn't realize it until I wrote it

August now   apples have started
                              severing from the tree
over the deck   by night their dim impact
                              thuds into dreams
by daylight bruised   starting to stew in sun
saying "apple" to nose and tongue
                              to memory

        Word following sense, the way it should be
and if you don't speak the word
                                do you lose your senses
And isn't this just one speck, one atom
                        on the glazed surface we call
America
        from which I write
                the war ghosts treading in their shredded
                                disguises above the clouds
and the price we pay here still opaque as the fog
these mornings
                        we always say will break open?

II

Try this one on your tongue: "the poetry of the enemy"
If you read it will you succumb

Will the enemy's wren fly through your window
and circle your room

Will you smell the herbs hung to dry in the house
he has had to rebuild in words

Would it weaken your will to hear
riffs of the instruments he loves

rustling of rivers remembered
where faucets are dry

"The enemy's water"   is there a phrase
for that in your language?

And you   what do you write
now in your borrowed house   tuned in

to the broadcasts of horror
under a sagging arbor, *dimdumim*

do you grope for poetry
to embrace all this

—not describe, embrace   staggering
in its arms, Jacob-and-angel-wise?

III

Do you understand why I want your voice?
At the seder table it's said

you reclined and said nothing
now in the month of Elul is your throat so dry

your dreams so stony
you wake with their grit in your mouth?

There was a beautiful life here once
Our enemies poisoned it?

Make a list of what's lost but don't
call it a poem

that's for the scriptors of nostalgia
bent to their copying-desks

Make a list of what you love well
Twist it   insert it

into a bottle of old Roman glass
go to the edge of the sea

at Haifa where the refugee ships lurched in
and the ships of deportation wrenched away

IV

for Giora Leshem

Drove upcoast   first day of another year   no rain
oxalis gold lakes floating
on January green

Can winter tides off the Levant
churn up wilder spume?

Think Crusades, remember Acre
wind driving at fortress walls

everything returns in time except the
utterly disappeared
What thou lovest well can well be reft from thee

What does not change / is the will
to vanquish
the fascination with what's easiest
see it in any video arcade

is this what the wind is driving at?

Where are you Giora?   whose hands
lay across mine a moment
Can you still believe that afternoon
Talking   you smoking   light and shade
on the deck, here in California
our laughter, your questions of translation
your daughter's flute?

First published in *The School Among the Ruins: Poems 2000–2004* (New York: W. W. Norton & Co., forthcoming)

complicity

David Thorne

An unwillingness to speak means I'm good at policing myself. Letting the wrong thing slip could prove fatal. Certain things are better left unsaid. I'm willing to pull out my fingernails rather than give anything away. I'll burn my face and cut off an ear when the pressure's on. I'll scorch and disfigure my genitals when it comes down to it because I don't want to admit how much I know and what I've done. And when the silence gets unbearable I'll sever my head and throw my body into a ditch.

consumer

Jude Todd

Abysmal: extremely, hopelessly bad; of or pertaining to an **abyss.**

Abyss: hell; Hades; realm of the god **Pluto,** who opened a gaping maw in the Earth to trap and **consume** Persephone. Some say that the Iraq war is an abyss from which Americans cannot emerge. (See **americium; engulf; plutocracy; plutonium.**)

Americium: a man-made transuranic element produced by the high-energy helium bombardment of uranium and **plutonium.** Americium is found in weapons that employ depleted uranium (**DU**); ingesting the tiniest particle of americium can cause cancer (see **consumption**) and genetic defects. (See **abysmal; Pluto.**)

Consume: to eat; to use up; to devour. From the Latin *sumere,* "to take." The "con" in "consume" is not derived from the Latin *con/com* for "together," in which case it might mean communion, as in eating together, i.e., sharing; rather, this "con" means "altogether," or "wholly," so to consume is to *take wholly,* i.e., to **engulf.**

Consumer: one who **consumes;** an organism that feeds on others. 20 percent of the world's wealthiest humans consume 86 percent of its resources. U.S. Americans are particularly adept consumers; we currently **engulf** 30 percent of the Earth's natural resources. We also produce more **waste** per capita than any other country. (See **greed.**)

Consumer goods: objects produced to satisfy human desires, often without regard for the good of either human or non-human others. (See **greed.**)

Consumption: the act of consuming. An older use of "consumption" referred to tuberculosis and to a progressive **wasting** of the body. Contemporary consumption results in the wasting of the Earth's body and of the body politic of all nations. Wars waged to protect the U.S. consumptive lifestyle waste life. (See **DU; greed; Gulf War(s).**)

DU: depleted uranium, an extremely dense radioactive **waste** product of nuclear reactors, used in cluster bombs and other weapons in both **Gulf Wars.** DU is composed of uranium-238, neptunium, **plutonium,** and **americium,** all rolled into a hyper-dense ball of hell that burns on contact and causes cancer, neurological diseases, and genetic defects. In the first **Gulf War,** over 320 tons of DU were pounded into the Iraqi earth. The amount of DU used in Gulf War II is unknown. Because DU continues to kill long after its initial use, the United Nations considers DU a "weapon of indiscriminate use" and, therefore, a violation of the Geneva Conventions. (See **abysmal.**)

Engulf: to **consume;** to swallow up. (See **abyss; greed; gulf.**)

Greed: excessive desire for wealth. In many cultures, greed is understood to cause destruction, so their teachings guard against it. Even before the U.S. culture **consumed** this land, Pueblo Indians told stories of times when greed destroyed the world. (See **abysmal.**) In U.S. culture, however, greed is celebrated, and during a crisis it is especially prized. After the 9/11 attack, U.S. Americans were urged to fight that evil by buying more goods. (See **americium; Gulf War(s).**)

Gulf: a portion of sea partly enclosed in land; a deep hollow; an **abyss.** (See **Pluto.**)

Gulf War(s): wars started by George Bushes to preserve the consumptive lifestyle of the richest U.S. Americans. (See **abyss; americium; DU; engulf; greed; plutocracy.**)

Pluto: the Greek god who caused Persephone to be **engulfed** by an **abyss** in the Earth. Pluto imprisoned Persephone in Hades and **consumed** her, i.e., he raped her. The Earth shared Persephone's shock, terror, and grief; grains refused to grow and all life **wasted** away. Pluto tricked Persephone into eating a tiny particle, a pomegranate seed, so that she would spend half her life in hell. (See **abysmal; plutocracy; plutonium.**)

Plutocracy: government by the wealthy, i.e., those who own most of the goods, those most adept at **consumption.** (See **greed.**)

Plutonium: a man-made transuranic element used to make DU. Its half-life of 24,000 years ensures that plutonium will be highly toxic for hundreds of thousands of years. **Engulfing** even a tiny particle of plutonium can cause cancer/**wasting.** (See **abysmal; americium; consumption; Pluto.**)

Waste: By-product of **consumption.** (See **abysmal.**)

coronation

Lynn Randolph

democracy

James K. Rowe and Sean Burns

U.S. democracy—so often held up as a model around the world—is in trouble. Domestic authoritarianism (PATRIOT Acts 1 and 2) is being sold as democratic insurance, while bloody wars in Afghanistan and Iraq, and less than covert interventions in Venezuela and Haiti, are marketed as democratic promotion. The cherry on top is that most opinion-shapers in Bush's democracy-loving cabal (Rumsfeld, Rice, Wolfowitz, Ashcroft) were not democratically elected, including Bush himself.

The point is, however, that U.S. representative democracy has never been particularly democratic. The distance between representatives and the people ("the demos") established in the U.S. constitution—a distance registered in geographic space, the time between elections, and a generally inaccessible political process for ordinary citizens—enables the kind of accelerated abuse we are witnessing today. While it is clear the Bush Administration should be resisted on democratic grounds, the less obvious point is that U.S. democracy *itself* can be resisted on democratic grounds.

The Greek *demokratia* is often translated as "rule by the people." Yet there exists a more accurate and enabling translation: "power of the people." Instead of people handing their power over to rulers, the latter translation suggests that democracy is alive in moments when people create *themselves* as politically empowered agents, not as rulers or subjects, but as citizens capable of participating in their collective constitution.

At present democracy is strongest when practiced outside of formal political institutions. This is for the simple reason that the U.S. state was self-consciously forged to limit, not promote democracy (see Federalist

Paper No. 10). More than formal political institutions and traditional political theory, current and past social movements are democracy's richest archive. The simple lesson these movements teach is that democracy only becomes real when practiced by the demos itself.

The most impressive democratic movement at work today is the many-headed hydra known as the "global justice movement." The movement does not limit its struggle to the inclusion of more and more people in formal decision-making. What makes this movement truly democratic is that it seeks to both activate the people as decision makers and transform the decision making process itself.

The global justice movement—also known as the "movement of movements"—has a multitude of origin stories. While the 1994 Zapatista uprising in Chiapas is generally treated as the beginning of this round of struggle, others locate a beginning 150 years ago when working people became an international revolutionary movement, and still others find a beginning 510 years ago with indigenous resistance against Columbus. The threads weaving these struggles together are demands for collective self-determination that resist distant and unaccountable authority.

At stake in these histories of struggle is how much control ordinary people exercise over their lives. U.S. representative democracy was a compromise between the simple belief that all human beings are capable of democratic participation, and the more contemptuous claim that only a select few should be politically empowered. The global justice movement is refreshingly uncompromising; it does not simply want a more representative democracy. Instead the movement moves to reintroduce people to their power, to their capacity for collective constitution. "Bring power closer to home" writes the editorial collective of a recent collection on the global justice movement; "reduce the distance of decision-making and those the decisions affect—this is the demand that resonates from the valleys of Narmada to the plains of Ecuador, from the squatted European social centers to the spokescouncils of Seattle, from the township meetings in Durban to the neighborhood assemblies of Buenos Aires. The movement of movements demands power that is not on paper, that is not abstract nor far away, but exercised in our streets, our land, and our lives."[1] It is here in the heart of movements where we find democracy's fugitive history being nurtured through countless acts of political freedom.

---

[1]Notes from Nowhere (ed.), *We Are Everywhere: The Irresistible Rise of Global Anticapitalism* (London: Verso, 2003) 390.

dental

see **beard**

the disappeared
in prison

Angela Y. Davis

Desaparecidos is a term we associate with the practices of the military junta that seized power in Argentina in 1976. Thousands of people suspected of involvement with what the dictatorship labeled "left terrorism"—including opposition party members, labor activists, journalists, and engaged artists—vanished without a trace. It has been determined that many of them were held captive in a network of secret detention centers, where they became anonymous hooded prisoners, subject to humiliation, torture, and murder.

A quarter of a century later, photographs taken in a military detention center outside Baghdad, Iraq are placed in global circulation, thus revealing the ugly details of what may well have been the fate of the *desaparecidos* in Argentina. The victims, who are also purported to be "terrorists," probably include labor activists, journalists, and cultural workers, as well as opposition party members. Only the families, colleagues and friends of these twenty-first-century disappeared can tell us who they really are. But this time it is not a South American military dictatorship utilizing the well-preserved techniques of torture, but rather the military arm of a government that claims to represent the most advanced democracy in the world.

Camp X-Ray in the U.S. military base located in Guantánamo Bay, Cuba and Abu Ghraib in Baghdad, Iraq are only two of the prisons that comprise a secret network of U.S. military detention facilities outside the territories directly controlled by the U.S. government. It is also suspected that such facilities may exist on board ships and in such countries as Diego Garcia, Jordan, and Pakistan. Many thousands of purported terrorists are held captive in these places, where they have probably been subjected to the psychological and physical pain we know has been inflicted on prisoners in Guantánamo and Abu Ghraib.

Abu Ghraib and Guantánamo are imaginary and real social environments that correspond to the rhetorical violence associated with the Bush administration's "war on terror." In the rhetorical universe of the war on terror, whoever is labeled "terrorist" or "unlawful combatant"—a process, whose racial dimension is unambiguous—deserves treatment that is in violation of the Geneva Conventions and acknowledged international human rights standards.

But if Abu Ghraib and Guantánamo recall the fate of the *desaparecidos* in Argentina, they have also been enabled by techniques of incarceration that characterize normal operations in the vast network of U.S. domestic prisons. Both military detention facilities and domestic prisons constitute extreme sites where democracy has lost its claims. As traumatized as many people may have been by the release of photographs depicting physical, psychological, and sexual torture of prisoners in Iraq, there has been a general reluctance to explore the links between torture in the outfield and torture at home. What would it mean to consider the relationship between the disappeared who inhabit secret detention facilities and the disappeared who inhabit state and federal prisons, paying special attention to the relatively new supermaximum security regimes? Lack of human contact and sensory deprivation so completely deprive prisoners of agency that they are compelled to express themselves by throwing their own feces at the agents of control. These regimes of incarceration have been seemingly self-generated—in order to manage what are considered the "worst of the worst." Minimum security used to imply medium and maximum security. Now the minimum implies the supermaximum—and who knows what lies beyond the supermaximum. These regimes have enormous staying power, for they appear to have been self-generated by the process of classification, which adheres to the rule of democracy.

When Iraqi prisoners ask whether the recent evidence of torture furnishes material evidence of the kind of democracy the United States is determined to bring to the Middle East, this is a question that deserves to be taken seriously. For the rest of the world, the economy of images of U.S. democracy has shifted toward representations of hooded figures—recapitulating the practices of the early penitentiary, as well as contemporary sexual coercion that saturates women's and men's prisons. However, young white women apparently taking pleasure in forcing nude Iraqi men to masturbate is a strange but meaningful representation of the military as site for the production of gender equality. Now women can participate in torture on a basis of equality with men.

In the immediate aftermath of the release of the first images of Abu Ghraib, the French daily *Le Monde* published a cartoon depicting an enormous boot crushing the head of an Iraqi prisoner accompanied by the words, *"Repetez: DE-MO-CRA-TIE."* If we feel certain that Argentina's "dirty war" must never happen again, not here, there, or anywhere, precisely because it was fundamentally anti-democratic, what does it mean to acknowledge the repression, torture, and sexual coercion that constitute the underbelly of a particular version of democracy, which has achieved dominance in the world? But more importantly, what version of democracy do we want for the future and how can we guarantee that technologies of disappearance will cease to exist?

the disappeared
in silence

Wendy Coxshall

Political violence between Shining Path guerrillas[1] and the Peruvian armed forces devastated Peru from 1980 until September 12, 1992, when Shining Path was "defeated" on the capture of its founding leader, Abimael Guzmán Reynoso. Political violence was most intense in the Amazonian lowlands and Andes, and especially in Ayacucho, where the violence first emerged. Many outsiders have assumed that Andean people, especially from the highlands, are Shining Path "terrorists." Colonial structures of power persist in Peru, upholding the state and a racialized hierarchy of class and gender that organizes relations among people within Peru. Members of the "white" coastal elite and intellectuals within and outside Peru use the terms "Indian" and/or "peasant" to denote the "primitivism" and "inferiority" of Andean people, and especially Andean women.[2] Many of the urban poor in the Andes also use racialized class labels to mark their "superiority" over the rural poor. Shining Path and the Peruvian armed forces both employed *disappearing* as a deliberate tactic of violence that was mostly carried out on men. The Peruvian Truth and Reconciliation Commission (2001–03) was established to investigate political violence in Peru between 1980 and 2000. This includes political violence perpetrated by the Peruvian armed forces under the regime of ex-President Fujimori, who remains in exile in Japan, having fled charges of corruption and human rights violations against him in Peru.

Paulina and Mercedes are both widows whose husbands were *disappeared*. Paulina is also a mother whose son was *disappeared* when he was twenty-one years old. They both returned to their highland community in Ayacucho in 1994, after being displaced by political violence. "Have you met my son?" Paulina asked me. She is confident that her son is still alive and has been displaced while she believes her husband is dead because he was sick and dying when he was *disappeared*. "My son might be lost and unable to find his way home from the unfamiliar place in which he may have been dumped all that time ago," Paulina elaborated. This is not an irrational suggestion because death is not, necessarily, the final outcome of *disappearing;* what *disappearing* constitutes is ultimately uncertain.

Disappearing, a tactic of violence performed on persons who are *disappeared,* also has ongoing violent effects for the close kin they leave behind. Mercedes heard the Peruvian Truth and Reconciliation Commission declare on the radio that many "innocent" people are still imprisoned in Lima, in the aftermath of political violence. She suggested that her husband "may be among those prisoners if he was transported to Lima." However implausible this might be, Mercedes has no contradictory evidence to explain where her husband has gone and what has happened to him since he was *disappeared.* Mercedes and Paulina know their husbands were summoned, on separate occasions, to take firewood to the military barracks from which neither of them has ever returned. Paulina was told by "others" that her son *disappeared* after participating in a military parade when he was in town. But the military have always denied all knowledge of their husbands and Paulina's son.

The Peruvian Truth and Reconciliation Commission engaged in finding and excavating mass graves to return identified bodies of the *disappeared* to their living close kin as a way to reveal to them the "truth" about what happened to their loved ones. Commissioners aspire to facilitate the mourning processes, which have been impossible for these relatives without bodies to bury that might bring them final closure. But there can be no such "truth" for thousands of relatives of the *disappeared* like Paulina, who told me, "However much I want his bones to bury him properly and know where he is at last—if he is really dead—this would never be enough to end my struggle to find my son and enable him to return home. How could I be sure any bones I might be given really belong to my son and that he is not still alive somewhere? I would not recognize his bones, but I would recognize him immediately if he were to walk over that hill in the distance. Then, I would know he has finally come home."

Whether or not a body is found, the *disappeared* are not dead; rather, they are eternally "missing" persons, who may still be alive somewhere. The enduring pain that close kin of the *disappeared* suffer deserves and demands to be acknowledged by others, not least by the states who are most often responsible for carrying out these heinous acts of violence.

---

[1]A Marxist-Leninist-Maoist movement, formed by particular Peruvian intellectuals at the University of San Cristobal of Huamanga (Ayacucho), which was a split faction of the Peruvian Communist Party.

[2]Marisol de la Cadena, "Women are More 'Indian'" in B. Larsson, Olivia Harris, with Enrique Tandeter, eds., *Ethnicity, Markets and Migration in the Andes: At the Crossroads of History and Anthropology* (Durham: Duke University Press, 1995), 329.

economic recovery

Karen Z. Ho

Nostalgic for the late 1990s?
Proclaimed to be the greatest boom in U.S. history?
As measured by
Unprecedented corporate profits AND the longest
    rising stock market
As well as, surprise,
Record numbers of corporate downsizings
    and rampant job insecurity . . .

Pause: Notice the inverse correlation between how the stock market is doing at year-end (as measured by the Dow Jones Industrial Average) and the job cuts announced by major U.S. corporations (a very conservative estimate of downsizing, as it only counts those actually announced by large companies).

	Positions Cut*	Stock Market**
1995	439,882	5,117.12
1996	477,147	6,448.27
1997	434,350	7,908.25
1998	677,795	9,181.43
1999	675,132	11,497.12

*Data from Challenger, Grey, & Christmas
**Data from Dow Jones & Company

So, what kind of boom did we have?
A boom measured by the stock market
A boom fueled by job loss and
Fooled by low unemployment figures bolstered
    by Wal-Mart and Manpower jobs
A boom disconnected from people's lives:
One of the largest extractions of wealth from labor
    to the stock price and the shareholder

But, who was the shareholder?
We were told it was US.
We were told, it's okay to be downsized, at least your
    401K is rising.
(Of course, unless you own thousands of shares
    of stock AND have the capability of selling
    at the "right" time, who wouldn't prefer a steady,
    well-paying job?)
We were told we are all investors now—a nation
    of investors, a shareholder democracy.
Trade online for $9.95!

Is this what Jesse Jackson thought when he spoke
    to African-American communities in 1999?
"Stop investing in the bear lotto and get into
    the bull market!"
"Don't miss this chance," for
True freedom lies in economic opportunity
And the source of empowerment is the amazing
    stock market.

I wonder if Jackson realized that on Wall Street,
    financiers continued to declare,
"When the taxicab driver starts to talk to you
    about stocks, take it as a sign
To sell."
(Insiders get out, and the last to "invest" are left
    holding the bag.)
Don't believe the hype? It was too late.
Now that Wall Street is US, who could we blame
    but ourselves for corporate decisions, for job
    insecurity, for our economic boom, for being
    invested in the new American Dream . . .

Imploding by 2000
Even for middle-class shareholders
How could it be otherwise?
When the art of the boom sets the stage for the bust?
When you merge, acquire, cut research and development,
    slash labor, whatever it takes to boost
The Stock Price
When you mortgage the future of the company
    for the quick spike
When volatility and cashing out on the UP
    is the name of the game
Who's left to take care of the long term?

And, now, W (has he "recovered" from his drunken
    stupor?) has declared

The economy is growing; we are in an economic recovery
What will it be measured by this time?

end, exit, return

Raymond Apthorpe

If the *end of war* announced by George W. Bush from
the deck of that aircraft carrier on May 1, 2003 was the
end of anything, certainly it was not the end of the war.
It was perhaps the end of *awe* in Iraq, but even earlier Iraqi resistance had emerged. Compared with awe,
shock was longer lasting—though not where the Rumsfeld brigade said it would be. Rather it was the millions *outside* Iraq who, well before the war began, first
were shocked to imagine that anyone reckoning its likely anti-humanitarian cost could actually be in favor of
it, then further shocked to think that it might actually
come to pass, and then even more shocked to see that
it was pursued as it was, with its commanders blam-
ing "terrorists" for "violent, extreme" action, as if their
own actions were not. Meanwhile, hardly a media com-
mentator was taking the slightest exception to this war
waged through *words* of mass deceit and destruction.

What is an "end"? In this case a continuing objective that was far from having been achieved, wrapped
for the media though it was as a mercy mission done
and over. Exit? In Iraq certainly not a termination, nothing like a wind-up and out. This war's lack of *exit strategy* is but another of its amazing, numbing features. Not
that various other and earlier interventions called humanitarian (what has been learned from them?) were
better supplied in this regard. What *didn't* depart with
proconsul Bremer when his brought-forward "use-by"
date arrived in June 2004, exactly as laid down in edicts

and as fully intended by the occupiers, is much more substantive and important than just who or what did quit: the continuing if hastily redesigned institutional imperial props for dispossession in the name, of course, of "freedom." The *return* of sovereignty is anyway a very strange way of talking about something that has been violated but can never be fully taken away. The mirage of "return" is another deceit intended to turn attention from the brutality of the *entrance.*

Any triumphalism dragged out of this war will be for the *un*-willing, who predicted these very woes.

face

Yasushi Uchiyamada

She stares back at the camera with slightly frightened eyes, a morsel of food clutched between her thumb and index finger, poised, waiting. Her right arm is all bones and skin. The face of this African infant, facing down the lens's eye, adorns the front cover of UNICEF's *Adjustment with a Human Face,* published in 1987. It is not the first appropriation of the human face, nor the last. A decade later, UNICEF published *Development with a Human Face,* and then in 1999, *Globalization with a Human Face.*

The global development industry presses the face to its own service. The face of the aid industry—*aid . . . industry*—is a mask. The face is a hiding place, configured to conceal the inhumane aspects of state-making and imperial agendas. It is not only the United Nations that lives inside this masquerade.

Japan, a leading bilateral aid donor, attaches a face to its assistance, not only to give it a more human—*humane*—appearance, but to ensure that its "beneficiaries" recognize the face of the patron. "Assistance with the visible face of our country": it's a national advertisement.

The *Field Service Code* of the Imperial Army tells us:

> The battlefield is where the Emperor's Army, acting under the Emperor's command, displays its divine essence . . . so that the enemy may look up in awe to the august dignity of the Emperor's nation.

Today Japanese soldiers join the U.S. President's war in Iraq. Aid recipients are expected to gaze in

Japanese soldiers test water quality
in Samawa, Iraq on March 7, 2004

awe—perhaps even gratitude—at the faceless national face of a formal and empty patriotism. The Prime Minister says Japan must help the United States help the people of Iraq. Yet the people of Iraq are increasingly at war with the occupying force. Japanese soldiers are in Iraq, we are told, to provide humanitarian aid. *Military occupation with a human face.*

family

Helene Moglen

The United States government has the weakest family support policies in the industrial world. It also employs the strongest possible rhetoric to defend the family in its nuclear form and to caution against its alterations and demise. Although the hypocrisy of the government is obvious, that obviousness is, to some extent, misleading. Fetishizing the family is more than a strategy of the political and religious Right. Across the ideological and socioeconomic spectrum, people are invested in grandiose images of an institution that has ceased to be tenable for a range of cultural and economic reasons.

The modern nuclear family appeared in the U.S. less than two centuries ago as an innovation of the developing middle classes. A new division of labor, encouraged by shifts in the capitalist economy, separated a masculine public world from a feminized private sphere. The family was detached and isolated as an economic and affective unit. Entrepreneurial fathers provided economic support while dependent mothers managed intrafamilial relations, which were emotionally charged and psychically fraught. Through the long period of industrialization, these arrangements were maintained by the exploited (and disavowed) labor of racial, socioeconomic and ethnic others. The normative family naturalized social differences that were hierarchically arranged while it produced psychic bonds that were strong enough to ensure the nuclear family's reproduction. For the part of the twentieth century in which men were able to earn an adequate family wage, significant sectors of the working class participated in this structure.

Today's discourse of family values assumes that we live our increasingly post-industrial lives in an early industrial world that requires the continuation of modern domestic arrangements. Of course, every aspect of this assumption is dramatically incorrect. In this postmodern moment, the nature of the middle classes, of gender and gender relations, of marriage and therefore of the family, have all been radically changed. With the wealth of 1 percent of households exceeding the combined wealth of the 95 percent that remains, the shape of the middle class has been startlingly reconfigured.[1] As more middle- and working-class families cling to the margins of economic security, they find that safety nets have disappeared. With two wage earners needed for some families to prosper and for others to survive, few adults remain at home. Child care poses agonizing problems to which there are usually individualized, precarious and unsatisfying solutions. The institution of the family is crumbling under the weight of job losses, wage cuts, inadequate health and child care, and the excision of federal assistance and family subsidy programs. Conditions known before by the poor have become familiar to those who were once comfortably situated in the middle. The State functions with willful disregard of these realities, concerned with the well-being of corporations and obsessed with its entrepreneurial war on terrorism, which drains resources from a domestic sphere that is—like the nation itself—hopelessly embattled.

The achievements of feminism, one of the most successful emancipatory movements of the twentieth century, have contributed decisively to the nuclear family's transformation. In response to economic pressures, and with feelings of entitlement, women enter the work force in unprecedented numbers, at all professional and socioeconomic levels. In this way, the modern gender division of labor has lost its relevance—and the normative nuclear family has lost its core. In the modern middle-class marriage, the ideology of romantic love veiled the psychological distance that gender difference created as well as the radical restrictions that marriage imposed upon women. In the revised social, legal and sexual environment of the post-modern marriage, women respond more actively to the failure of the romantic delusion. Greater gender equality produces different expectations, more independence, and greater freedom of choice. Between 40 and 50 percent of marriages now end in divorce[2] and only half of U.S. children live in nuclear families that include two biological parents.[3] Varied forms of family proliferate as people divorce, cohabitate, remarry, live alone and construct extensive networks of family and friends. The families that children experience as "theirs" may be quite different from those that each of their biological parents recognizes. For increasing numbers of people, kinship relations can be defined as those of "enduring, diffuse solidarity," and these include shifting clusters of people who are variously important at different stages of life.[4] These new familial clusters, which are assembled from various racial, ethnic, national, socioeconomic, and sexual groups, are broadly inclusive and represent the hybridization of identity that has become a fact of our daily lives.

Instead of recreating the inflexible structure that the modern nuclear family established, therefore, feminists are modifying it and inventing alternatives, some of which share the social flexibility and responsiveness of pre-modern kinship arrangements. But even as the institution of the family is transformed, there is fear and suspicion of the creative opportunities that some of these changes afford. Many who would distance themselves from the Moral Majority, and reject assumptions of the family-values crowd, share the nostalgic desire to return to the idealized nuclear family of the past. The rush of lesbian and gay partners to marry can be seen as an example of this regressive movement. Xenophobia, misogyny, homophobia, and racism contribute to the political effort to keep the nostalgic dream alive, but that dream is also nurtured by libidinal attachments that the nuclear family has functioned so well to create. The place where desire was shaped, satisfied and thwarted remains a mystified place that we have lost and to which we wish to return. This melancholic urge forces us to deny psychic and social realities that call outmoded family values into question. Once we acknowledge these realities, we can begin to resist the paralyzing ideology of the normative nuclear family, and we can start to explore the liberating possibilities that modified and alternative domestic arrangements provide.

---

[1]Jeff Gates, "Modern Fashion or Global Fascism," *Tikkun* 17.1 (Jan/Feb 2002), 3–6.

[2]Stephanie Coontz, *The Way We Really Are: Coming to Terms with America's Changing Families* (New York: Basic Books, 1997), 31.

[3]Coontz, 79.

[4]David Schneider, *American Kinship: A Cultural Account* (Englewood Cliffs, NJ: Prentice-Hall, 1980 [1968]), 52.

family of patriots

NeEddra James

Vanity Fair magazine has produced photographic representations of the White House during wartime since the First World War. In February 2002 the magazine continued that dubious tradition with its "War and Destiny" cover story, reproduced below.[1] The lush and glamorous collection of images introduces readers to all of the significant players on "Team Bush": "The Commander-in-Chief [G. W. Bush]," "The Rock [Dick Cheney],"

"The Conscience [Colin Powell]," "The Confidant [Condoleezza Rice]," "The Protector [Tom Ridge]," "The Heat [John Ashcroft]" and of course, "The Secretary of War [Donald Rumsfeld]." While the magazine narrativizes the war and its principal figures in terms of sport or, from another angle, as if it were a film, one might also consider the ways in which the cover photograph mimics traditional family portraiture, yet updated for the "New American Century."

Family portraiture was a quite popular medium of visual representation in nineteenth-century U.S. culture. As a modality through which notions of normative bourgeois familial formations were represented, the family portrait also operated as a visual technology that replicated the racialized heteropatriarchal arrangement of the modern nation-state. *Vanity Fair*'s cover photo mobilizes some of the key features of family portraiture. The family of patriots are pictured in a sitting room, fireplace and painting located just behind them. Some members of the family sit, while others stand, but all are meant to flank the central character: the president-patriarch who is situated at the center of the image with an open suit jacket revealing a white shirt that contrasts with the dark attire of his extended family. Unlike its antecedents, non-white persons enter this family portrait not as nannies and butlers (though their "team" appellations—the conscience and confidant—are eerily reminiscent of former figures), but as integral members of the family of patriots *qua* family of Man, thereby marking the nation's ostensible achievement of an anti-racist, anti-sexist society. *Vanity Fair*'s portrait of the Bush Administration thus represents an aestheticized post-9/11 multicultural and gender-balanced U.S. national identity. Yet, this depiction of a perfected U.S. national identity does not render obsolete processes of identity formation that proceed by negation. To be sure, the family of patriots is not without an "Other."

The image to the right recuperates a familiar pop culture icon in a new form.[2] The spectral figure from the 1983 blockbuster film *Ghostbusters* returns as the CIA-DCI Counterterrorist Center's logo: *Terrorist-Buster.* The logo operates within the logic of caricature, which historically, was never too far away from allegedly "accurate" scientist modes of representation. In fact, racial/cultural caricature and illustration often translated anthropometric and ethnological photographs into cartoon images that sketched the excesses of alterity and exaggerated the differences between the normative viewing subject and the racialized specimen. However, with the alleged resolution of racialized subjugation and subsequent transformation of the U.S. into a multicultural neoliberal democracy, another strategy of representational dehumanization emerges.

The "terrorist-buster" is a ghostly, amorphous, nonhuman figure whose gender, racial and ethnic ambiguity enables its mobilization as a sign of generalized nonnormativity—but most importantly, as a sign of the monstrous terrorist. As a caricatured representation of radical alterity the image functions to visually designate the unpredictable and fluctuating nature of an undefinable national threat that haunts the country daily. The gaiety with which *Vanity Fair* celebrates wartime Washington obfuscates the concomitant production of an enemy-combatant that is porous by definition, and therefore could literally be anyone, anywhere, anytime. In this way, the scene *Vanity Fair* stages on its cover covers over the simultaneous constitution of a "them" always already posited as the antithesis of the collective "us." As Wahneema Lubiano has noted in another context: "Cover stories cover or mask what they make invisible with an alternative presence; a presence that redirects our attention, that covers or makes absent what has to remain unseen if the seen is to function as the scene for a different drama."[3]

---

[1]Christopher Buckley and Annie Leibovitz, "War and Destiny: The White House in Wartime," *Vanity Fair* 498 (February 2002).

[2]CIA/DCI Counterterrorist Logo, "Terrorist-Buster" (www.cia.gov/terrorism/buster.html).

[3]Wahneema Lubiano, "Black Ladies, Welfare Queens and State Minstrels: Ideological War by Narrative Means," in Toni Morrison, ed., *Race-ing Justice, En-gendering Power* (New York: Pantheon Books, 1992), 324.

fear

Afsaneh Kalantary

My fears—like yours—are multiple and accented. They take on the layering of personal and collective histories of exile and displacement, education and imperial conquests and wars. They have been formed and amassed in my multiple scatterings across the earth—a condition I share with millions of other people. My fears have opened my heart to many stories of violent displacement.

In my "preliterate" years, as an Azeri-speaking child growing up in Iran, my childish apprehensions were called *gorkhu.* My trepidations for the sound of thunder, the shifting of the earth, the darkness at night, the power of adults with their large stature towering over me, and most of all *Allah's* omnipresence were all *gorkhu.* Then again, as I became "cultured" and steeped in the formal language of schooling, I learned to say *gorkhu* in Farsi: *tars. Tars* entered my imaginary and my writings, and it became my literary expression of feeling *gorkhu.* My youthful *gorkhu*—from the Shah's secret service, *SAVAK,* and later Khomeini's *SAVAMA,* and my fright of both these rulers' dungeons and their systematic regimens of torture of their dissenters—was expressed as *tars,* albeit hidden in my gesture of youthful bravado.

Later, as I fled Iran and crossed the border to Turkey, my uncertainties about my future and my fretfulness at the threat of being caught by the Turkish authorities and sent back to Iran, were dubbed as *korku;* thanks to the shared Turkic roots of my native tongue with Turkish language, I was quite adept in translating my sentiments from *tars* to *korku.* Later, as I became a refugee in France, my *gorkhu* or *tars* did not subside, but yet again it shifted its familiar linguistic terrain and was christened as *peur.* I did not stay in France long enough for the hegemonic anti-immigrant sentiments to sediment my *peur.* As I finally settled in the U.S., yet again as a refugee, my *gorkhu, tars, korku,* and *peur* were baptized *fear.*

While in the States, as a resident alien (apparently a creature from outer space, that is, the Third World, the Middle East, and worse yet, Iran), I had many opportunities to flaunt my newly acquired fluency in my anglicized *gorkhu.* Whereas the nationally sanctioned and commonly expressed American fears were those of crime, aging, getting fat, communism, colored and poor immigrants, the decline of U.S. imperial power, and finally terrorism, I had my own unspoken fears. I learned: the *fear* of accounting for the "origin" of my accent; the *fear* of not finding a stable place in the hierarchy of colored people; and, at the same time, the *fear* of being blended in the American melting pot; and, yet again, not having the right to be different, in my own way; and the *fear* of joining the masses of unemployed and homeless "natives," ironically in the richest country on earth. Eventually, getting acclimated to my fears, I was *naturalized* to become a *naturally* fearful citizen. In this long and arduous process of savoring my transformation from an alien to a citizen, I entered other unknown worlds of utterances, and in pursuit of my personal and academic interests, I added *miedo* and *Angst* to my lexicon of fright.

Many a time, as a "legal" immigrant, I shared the *miedo* of multitudes of "illegal" immigrants in the

States as well as the *Angst* of the *Ausländer* (foreigners) in Germany. Ever since, *gorkhu, tars, korku, peur, miedo, Angst* and *fear* have colored the landscape of my adult apprehensions. I express my wakeful nightmares in a peculiar assortment of broken languages and in constant translation. As I dread these politically fraught moments in U.S. history, I experience my trepidations for a permanent state of war *and* terror as multiple layers of historically situated *gorkhu, tars, korku, peur, fear, miedo* and *Angst*.

fences

Dalit Baum and Lisa Rofel

The Zoo

The Biblical Zoo in Jerusalem has a special fence. Zoo officials explain: "The construction of the separation wall between the chimpanzees and the visitors has been completed. Contrary to the rest of the world, the fence is meant to protect the visitors, since in Jerusalem the chimpanzees used to throw stones at them."

Jerusalem Biblical Zoo, *Annual Report 2001* (www.jerusalemzoo.org.il)

Landscape

"The relationship between the landscape and the Israeli-Palestinian conflict is symbiotic. The terrain dictates the nature, intensity and focal points of confrontation, while the conflict itself is manifested most clearly in the processes of transformation, adaptation, construction and obliteration of the landscape and the built environment."

Rafi Segal and Eyal Weizman, eds., *A Civilian Occupation* (Tel Aviv/New York: Verso, 2003)

Wall and Tower

In 1987, Sharon Rotbard returned to his Paris architectural class with the fruits of his summer assignment: he had built a model of Kibbutz Tel Amal, the acclaimed prototype for settlements built in Palestine during the 1930s. This settlement system, named *Homa Umigdal* or Wall and Tower, holds a mythical status in the State of Israel as a symbol of sacrifice and heroism. The teacher took one look at something that Rotbard had, until that moment, had fond memories of, and exclaimed: "What is this Gulag?"

Homa Umigdal was a communal, fortified settlement, seemingly defensive, but whose objective was to seize control of land. "The system was based on the hasty construction of a wall made of prefabricated wooden molds filled with gravel and surrounded by a barbed wire fence. . . . Erected within this enclosure were a prefabricated wooden tower that commanded the surrounding area and four shacks that were to house a "conquering troop" of forty people. Between 1936 and 1939, some fifty-seven such outposts were set up throughout the country, outposts which rapidly developed into permanent settlements of the kibbutz and moshav type."

Sharon Rotbard, "Wall and Tower *(Homa Umigdal)"* in Rafi Segal and Eyal Weizman, eds., *A Civilian Occupation* (Tel Aviv/New York: Verso, 2003)

The Good Fence

After years of funding and arming the Christian Phalanges in the Lebanon civil war, Israel invaded Lebanon in 1982, put a siege on its capital, Beirut, and supported the massacre of thousands of Palestinians in Sabra and Shatila refugee camps. Israel maintained a violent military occupation in South Lebanon for eighteen years, using a local militia group called the South Lebanon

Army. During the occupation, a border crossing opened in the otherwise sealed border between Israel and Lebanon. This border crossing allowed Israel to sell goods in Lebanon, and to employ south Lebanese—if they had family members in the South Lebanon Army. This border crossing was called the Good Fence.

Security Fence

In June 2001, the Israeli government decided to erect a physical barrier to prevent the entry of Palestinians from the West Bank into Israel and Israeli major settlements. In most areas, the barrier is comprised of an electronic fence with dirt paths, barbed-wire fences, and trenches on both sides, at an average width of 180 feet. In urban areas, cutting through east Jerusalem and surrounding Palestinian cities like Qalkiliya, the barrier is a twenty- to twenty-five-foot-high wall, made of concrete slabs. The planned barrier will separate Palestinian population centers in the West Bank into three main areas, and will leave most of the fertile farmland and water sources on the Israeli side.

The Israeli state claims that Article 23(g) of the 1907 Hague Regulations allows for the seizure of private property when it is "imperatively demanded" by the necessities of self-defense.

From the Israel Ministry of Defense official website:

The underlying principle is to make it visually clear that this is an impenetrable space, so that anyone trying to cross it could be defined "a potential terrorist." Shooting regulations will be changed accordingly.

It should be noted that landscape architects were part of the planning team and their recommendations were taken into account in the decision making process concerning the route, in order to minimize damage to the landscape and its vegetation. . . . This same . . . "green" thinking is reflected in a special operation conducted in an area where a unique plant grows. Thousands of Iris bulbs were dug from the planned Security Fence and replanted outside it in order to preserve the beauty of the Iris.

Israeli Ministry of Defense (www.securityfence.mod.gov.il)

Letter from the Women of the Village of Biddu

The women's demonstration today is a peaceful protest against Israel's construction of the Apartheid Wall, which we consider a terrible Israeli plan to seize Palestinian land, expel thousands of Palestinian residents from their homes and transfer them. This Apartheid Wall will deprive the Palestinian people of their right to have their own state. The building of this wall will also prevent students from reaching schools and universities, the sick from reaching hospitals, farmers from reaching their land and workers from reaching their work. The Wall will further Israel's efforts to acquire and control water resources. All of Israel's actions, from seizing land to depriving residents of basic humanitarian services, is in clear violation of the Geneva Conventions and all international laws relating to people under military occupation.

Signed,
Women from the Village of Biddu,
NW Jerusalem District

The villagers of Biddu continue their daily nonviolent protests near the construction site of the fence, which will cut them off from almost all of their lands. So far, five peaceful protesters have been killed by the Israeli army in Biddu.

Good Fences Make Good Neighbors

In the village of Mas'ha, one family's home is surrounded by the 25-foot-tall concrete wall. The home was separated from the village after their yard became the site of resistance activities to the wall's construction. Israeli

Defense Forces now have to open and close the gate to let their children go to school.

According to existing plans, about 875,600 Palestinians (38 percent of the West Bank Palestinian population) will be either locked in enclaves surrounded by the barrier, or cut off from their farmland, workplaces or health services. About 235,750 acres of land (16.8 percent of the West Bank) will be either expropriated from Palestinians for the construction, surrounded by the barrier in enclaves, or left on the western side of the barrier, cut off from the rest of the West Bank.

B'Tselem—an Israeli Human Rights Organization, March 2004 (www
.btselem.org)

fire

Annemarie Mol

The slow burning of the living body: breathe in air; absorb oxygen; burn the food that has turned into you. Get hot.

It is not easy to look at a flame. One moment there is something to stare at; the next there is not. Here something is present; there not. This is why a space where absence and presence alternate may be called a fire space.

The biochemistry textbook tells: *Two molecules of ATP* [adenosine triphosphate] *are generated in the conversion of glucose to pyruvate.* In this sentence glucose is present. So is ATP, storing energy in a form that makes it readily available for immediate use by the cell. Absent, however, is the food you ate and turned into glucose; the oxygen required for its conversion into pyruvate; the experiments during which this sentence was painstakingly formulated. Absent they are; but without them the sentence could not have been written. So they are present as well. Absent/present.

Absent/present is a lot of history. The history of "glucose" that depends on the extraction of sugar from sugar cane. The orderly plantations where the cane was planted. The Africans sent across the ocean to work those plantations as slaves. Sweat, blood. The canal houses in Amsterdam built with the money thus earned. The Amerindians who lost their land or their lives. Ships, storms, scurvy. Sweet tea. Yet there they are in the biochemistry textbook: visible in the flames of its absent/present fire space. As are the laboratories with their test tubes and the technicians counting molecules of ATP.

The world is burning. Look at the flames in the fire space. In factory food, meanwhile, sugar from cane has been replaced by corn syrup; corn-based *fructose* has taken the lead over cane-based *glucose.* The corn is grown in the United States; cane plantations are mostly elsewhere these days. Fructose is less rapidly used and more readily stored by the body. Its burning is deferred in the fat of class-marking weight gain.

Burn, burn. Keep on breathing. The less energy a cell has available, the more easily it converts the available glucose into pyruvate. Some of us get too fat out of poverty. Others get too thin. Running to stay alive, they burn themselves up. Hungry, one may hope to find something to eat. Where is it? Where on earth?

There is so much absent and yet present in any sentence. Such is the nature of a fire space. There is so much left unspoken and yet screaming you in the face.

global positioning systems

Neerja Vasishta

Palace

In the pink city of Jaipur, there is a palace. The day I was a tourist there, a haggard director was filming a scene for the next Bollywood flop in one of the main courtyards. The profession-al dancers and actresses laden with layers of period costume and plastic jewelry sat on the steps, bored, waiting for their cue while I joined other curious tourists milling around, staring.

An American tourist and his partner were among those taking photos of the filming and during one break, he approached one of the dancers, stooped down to her, and while his partner looked on, a frozen smile on her face, offered in a sweet voice: "I'll give you five rupees if I can take your picture."

The dancer looked up, bored. With a silent and slight gesture, she accepted. She stared into his camera, which he adjusted before taking his perfect shot. As soon as she heard the shutter, she rejoined the dreary atmosphere of her friends while he smiled and gave her a bill at arms' length. Equally annoyed at the worthlessness of the bill as with the lack of pockets in her heavy skirt, she took the bill and the tourist returned to his proud partner.

An Indian tourist with a white starched shirt and impeccably creased polyester pants approached the couple. He grasped his old manual camera with one hand even though it was securely strapped around his neck. He smiled at the American and gestured toward his partner. With a heavy accent, he asked the tourist a question: "Can I take a picture of your wife if I pay you a dollar?"

The offended tourist turned red before waving away the Indian: "No! You can't." He put his arm in front of his partner, shielding her from the detrimental effects of the camera rays and the Indian tourist took a step away from them. The couple looked for a way out and exited through one of the elaborate doorways while the bored dancers returned their gaze to the director, anticipating their cue.

Llama

Thousands of miles away, another tourist couple sat facing the strong Andean sun. The woman in the white linen shirt wiped the sweat off her forehead while the man next to her stole a glance at the umbrella on the table next to them, willfully ignoring the shade. They continued their discussion about their trip so far. The woman spoke.

"You know, I don't understand those women that walk the streets yelling at us to take their picture in exchange for some money. I never want to stop and take a photo of them. It makes me feel . . ."

"Quite annoyed about it. It's quite rude."

She nodded in agreement with his description.

"I'd much rather give money to people who are just asking for money straight out. Rather than someone who says 'take a photograph of me' and then charges me for it."

He looked at her. "Right."

"I mean, I could take a picture of them, but why? Just to go back home and show the picture to my friends what the other side of society is like: traditional clothes, hair in two braids, cute kids wearing bright colors carrying a newborn sheep? I think it's kind of abusive—it's like abusing the culture they have. When you see people in the hills wearing those clothes day to day and they're not trying to get money for it, that's a different thing. It's real and I would be fine with taking their photo in that case. But when they are here all dressed up with a llama trailing behind on a string . . . it's . . . it's . . ."

The man adjusted his sunglasses again. "Hmm . . . yes."

glory

Anna Tsing

When Humpty Dumpties emerge across the spectrum of imperial endeavor, and, indeed, take on presidential guise, we might savor the words of the original:

> "There's glory for you!"
>
> "I don't know what you mean by 'glory,'" Alice said.
>
> Humpty Dumpty smiled contemptuously. "Of course you don't—till I tell you. I meant 'there's a nice knock-down argument for you!'"

"But 'glory' doesn't mean 'a nice knock-down argument,'" Alice objected.

"When I use a word," Humpty Dumpty said, in rather a scornful tone, "it means just what I choose it to mean—neither more nor less."

"The question is," said Alice, "whether you can make words mean so many different things."

"The question is," said Humpty Dumpty, "which is to be master—that's all."[1]

Remember, of course, to ask about the king's horses.

---

[1]Lewis Carroll, *Through the Looking Glass* (London: Oxford University Press, 1971), 190.

the green lady

P. A. Ebron

How is a climate of fear created? From an early age, many of us learn to be afraid of phantoms. Our childhood fears are revitalized in campaigns against fearful Others: black people, terrorists, Muslims, foreign spies, communists. But some of us *are* black. I am puzzled by the unreflective patriotism of so many African Americans who, like myself, are subjects of racial profiling—and yet follow their leaders to extend it to others.

• • •

Every day a group of us, mostly girls, would meet in the schoolyard during recess. We were all in the third grade in an all-black school. We would talk and play, all of us, that is, except Evelyn who had a tentative status with the group because she liked to start fights. For fifteen or twenty minutes we had a chance to be in the world according to kids. No teachers; only safety monitors managed several grades of students at the same time. During recess some of us entertained ourselves with dodgeball or games such as "squeeze the lemon," the favorite. Everyone in the game, maybe ten or twelve of us, would form a long line and push against the person in front, who'd push up against the person in front of him or her. We pressed against an insulated pipe that was on the outside of a set of new classrooms. The point of the game was to stay in the line all mashed in and not get squeezed out; if you hung in long enough, you might be at the front of the line. If you got squeezed out then you'd have to just stand in the cold and make remarks from the sidelines. No one wanted to stand outside the group. We were in this together.

At the far end of the schoolyard, perpendicular to one of the exits, was the sidewall of an adjacent house. The house had three stories that loomed ominously above us. At the top was a small attic window.

Johnny Durham, the class entertainer, happened to spend a little time with my friends before he was sent to reform school. Johnny was notorious for his offenses, and he had run out of allowable suspensions. He didn't just use "foul" language; he also ran into the girls' bathroom and opened all the doors to make the girls scream. Worse yet, he had played show-and-tell with a real gun, and, most recently, held up a bread truck. As his transgressions piled up, Johnny's stature grew. He captivated all the kids. He was like someone on television, but real. We admired his ability to stand up to anyone. He was funny, cool, daring, and fearless. He made the dull moments of school—of which there were many—bearable. Most of us were prepared to believe anything he said.

"There is a *green lady* who lives up there," he told us as he pointed to the small window at the top of the looming three-story house. None of us saw anything in that window—at least at first. But every day Johnny would add a detail. One day the green lady would be turned to the right, or she would be standing up but had leaned down to press her nose against the glass. She was too tall, he said, to stand up straight and look out the window. As he added details, a delegation of kids would go and look up to see if we could glimpse her.

Within a few days, some of us began to see her. At first it was just for a fleeting moment. Our descriptions were vague. "I think she was just passing by, but she was *there*."

"She was more gray than green," someone reported.

"She has kind of scraggly hair," someone else said, "and it's not combed." The Green Lady's main goal in life, according to Johnny Durham, was to terrorize little kids who bothered her by their stares up at her window. The Green Lady hated the noise from the schoolyard.

Within a week, more of us could see her. We were fully convinced that she was there. We grew so scared that she might one day get out and get us that we stopped using the exit that was close to her house. Johnny, before his departure, had left us with the scary news that the Green Lady would come out sometime around three o'clock, a half-hour before school let out. We worried that she might be late getting back one day, and she might grab one of us. All during the spring, we avoided that side of the schoolyard. When a carnival was held there, some of the most fun activities took place next to that back exit, but those of us certain of the Green Lady's existence avoided going to the booths in that area. She would really be angry about the noise then.

I remember this story every time I feel the anxiety created by U.S. anti-terrorist campaigns. Johnny Durham tells us once again that terrorists are near at hand. Is today's alert yellow, orange, or red? So convincing are these stories that some people find themselves afraid to travel next to those with certain racial, national, or religious looks. U.S. Americans are scared of their neighbors. Who circulated the characteristics that mark these Others in the first place? There is no reform school for those august leaders whose acts are so far beyond child's play. Yet the U.S. government's vigilant campaign against "weapons of mass destruction" has turned out to be no more substantial than the Green Lady.

Guernica

Sven Lindqvist

The bomb was first used by the Chinese a thousand years ago. . . . As long as the bomb was dropped at the enemy from the city wall, it was considered just a primitive forerunner to the rocket. But when it could be delivered from an aircraft, the power of the bomb became obvious.

The Italians started it on November 1, 1911 when they dropped the first bomb over Tagiura in Libya. The Spaniards came a close second. On December 17, 1913, captains Eduardo Barón and Carlos Cifuentes attacked the village of Ben Carich in Spanish Morocco, dropping four "Carbonit" shrapnel bombs filled with explosives and steel balls, to punish rebellious villages.

Bombing "savage" civilians soon became standard practice of colonial warfare. One example was the bombing of Tetuan on June 29, 1924, when twenty Spanish planes dropped 500 bombs causing large civilian losses. The worst atrocity was committed in 1925 against the "Guernica" of Morocco, Xauen, by American airmen in the service of France and Spain. "A number of absolutely defenseless women and children were massacred and many others were maimed and blinded," wrote the London *Times.*

In September the German consulate in Tetuan reported that Moroccan rebel villages were now being punished with mustard gas. Gas, as a weapon of mass destruction, was forbidden by the 1925 Geneva Convention. In the summer of 1925, the Red Cross requested permission to send weapons inspectors to the war zone to investigate reports of a gas war. The Spanish refused. But two German officers were invited to serve with the Spanish air force "in order to get experience, particularly in the use of gas in air warfare." In a secret report the Germans wrote that "Spain was primarily dependent on the result of systematic air attacks and the devastating effect of poison gas."

Of all these bombed towns and villages, most of them in Africa, the Middle East or the Far East, only one went down in history: Guernica. After all, Guernica lies in Europe. . . .

Already at the Hague Conference 1899 many participants feared a future "Guernica." The small countries argued for a total prohibition of air war. The then superpower, Great Britain, opposed prohibition: "It can be proved to the hilt that scientific development of engines of destruction had tended a) to make nations hesitate before going to war; b) to reduce the percentages of losses in war; c) to shorten the length of campaigns, and thus to reduce to a minimum the sufferings endured by the inhabitants."

All through the twentieth century these three arguments were repeated over and over again, in support of weapons, systems able to achieve not only a new "Guernica," but a million new "Hiroshimas."

The fourth Hague Convention of 1907, which is still valid international law, states in article 25 that "bombardment by whatever means of towns, villages, dwellings, or buildings which are undefended, is prohibited."

This Convention was systematically violated by all parties of World War II, especially by the British over Germany and the Americans over Japan. Immediately after the war the International Red Cross tried to restore the laws of war protecting civilians. But the victorious powers could hardly agree to such laws without incriminating themselves for what they had just done and planned to continue doing.

The French bombed Madagascar, Vietnam, Algeria. The British bombed Malaysia, Aden, Kenya. The U.S. bombed Korea and Vietnam. Perceived as Communist or terrorist threats, movements for independence were for three decades bombed all over the non-European world, creating innumerable "Guernicas."

The U.S. and Britain skillfully and energetically worked against Red Cross efforts to protect civilians. Not until the decolonization process was over was a new convention finally accepted on June 10, 1977. It was for the first time truly international. It applied to all continents, to all political systems and to both external and internal conflicts. The basic rule says:

"The Parties to the conflict shall at all times distinguish between the civilian population and combatants and between civilian objects and military objectives and accordingly shall direct their operations only against military objectives."

Article 51 expressly prohibits the use of any weapon whose effects cannot be limited to a specific military objective.

Can these paragraphs prevent another "Guernica"? Yes, they could—but only if international law is backed by the forceful support of public opinion all over the world.

Every time international law is violated with impunity, be it in the World Trade Center, in Afghanistan or in Iraq, its protective power is reduced everywhere. But the opposite is also true. International law is gaining power to protect us every time it is upheld by us, against the violators—be it in New York, in Afghanistan, in Iraq or anywhere in the world.

hair

see **beard**

homeland
in the U.K.

Marilyn Strathern

Chilling.
A word for now: I could have sworn we never talked
    that way.

It was Home Office (for everything not foreign
    or specialist), not Homeland Office;
Home not Homeland Guard (local defense in WWII).

It must have existed before—
My Collins Dictionary has two short notes:

homeland 1. the country in which one lives or was born;
2. the official name for Bantustan

There you have it! From the occupation of Poland
    to ethnic cleansing!

Today, Homeland Security. Birthrights.
The dictionary also lies, then. Homeland is not where
    you live if you've travelled there.

An unsafe place, barbed.

homeland
in Hawai'i

Kathy E. Ferguson and **Phyllis Turnbull**

The U.S. "homeland" came into existence at a price—the theft of the homelands of others: the Mohican, Choctaw, Erie, Ute, Sioux, Seminole, Cree, Apache, Narragansett, Crow, Osceola, Algonquin, Potawotami, Ojibway, Cherokee, Mashpee, Sauk, Fox, Mohawk, Paiute, Seneca, Dakota, Chippewa, Pequot, Tejon, Digger, Massasoit, Wampanoag, Hopi, Salishan, Micmac, Iroquois, Yana, and the Hawaiian and others. Now, 200 years later, despite having the world's largest "defense" budget for decades, the U.S. now has a new security problem with its homeland: it can be blown up by shoes or airplanes.

The phrase "homeland security" suggests both perverse silence and, especially in Hawai'i, bitter irony. Since the late 1990s, and especially since September 11, 2001, "homeland security" has competed with "national security" as the prevailing alibi for hegemonic power. If, now, we are securing our homeland, then what exactly were we securing before? The nation, evidently, but how is that different from the homeland? The more sentimental and domestic reference to "home" implicitly contrasts with the larger, less personal, unspoken referent for "nation"—"national security" has come to mean U.S. operations anywhere on the globe (or, increasingly, in space) to enforce military and corporate power, while "homeland security" has a cozier ring to it, suggesting the securing of our safety right here in our own private place.

So our own private home turns out to be stolen. In 1893, a giant land grab in the Pacific brought the previously independent Hawaiian Kingdom under the possession of the United States. Hawai'i was initially stolen to serve as military outpost and refueling station for the United States. Continued expansion has included the development of Pearl Harbor and the seizure of immense tracts of land and water for bases and training facilities. Struggles by Native Hawaiian organizations to regain control of their stolen homeland, while seeing some successes, have largely failed to dislodge the overwhelming claims of U.S. national security.

Hawai'i is now experiencing another extensive land grab by the military:

- Expansion of Pacific Missile Range on Kaua'i by 270 acres, with added control of the surrounding 5,371 acres, at no charge to the federal government;

- Enlargement of existing bases and training facilities by 1400 additional acres on O'ahu (added to the 25 percent of the island already off limits to residents), and by 23,000 acres on the Big Island, including a 300 percent increase in army vehicle miles, to accommodate the organization and training of a $1.5 billion Stryker Brigade Combat Team;

- A proposed carrier air wing on O'ahu;

- Expansion of live-fire training in Makua Valley on O'ahu and at other sites.

Together these expansions increase the military's holdings by 12.8 percent, the biggest expansion in Hawai'i since World War II; more armaments make Hawai'i a more attractive target and thus makes people living here less secure. The environment is degraded, the culture militarized, and the economy pressured by military expansion. Meanwhile, military claims savage the ability of Native Hawaiians to articulate their own notion of homeland via their sovereignty movement.

human

see **chicken**

humanitarian intervention

see **weapons of mass destruction**

information and communication technologies

Warren Sack

There is a difference between transmission and communication. Transmission is successful between two people if the receiver can recreate and perhaps repeat the sender's message. In contrast, communication is successful between two people if some form of shared understanding is achieved. Thus, the email message in my inbox written in a language unknown to me constitutes a successful transmission, but an unsuccessful communication. This difference between transmission and communication explains why communication seems to be on the wane. In short, communication technologies as they are currently designed do not help us communicate with one another. Due to the misguided theory of communication-as-transmission, we now live in an information environment where local and international exchanges have been forced into the mold of transmission. Most so-called Information and Communication Technologies (ICTs) are neither information nor communication technologies. They are, instead, simply *bit transmission technologies* that need to be critically decompiled and rebuilt if they are ever to have any potential as communication technologies.

Symptomatic of the ICTs intended to support international communication is so-called "automatic translation" software. In 1949 one of the inventors of the mathematical theory of information and communication, Warren Weaver, wrote and distributed a report to two hundred of his colleagues. The title of Weaver's report was "Translation." Its purpose was to explore the idea that one might design a computer program to translate texts from one language to another. Anyone who has done the work of a translator is likely to find Weaver's understanding of translation fantastical:

> When I look at an article in Russian, I say, "This is really written in English, but it has been coded in some strange symbols. I will now proceed to decode."[1]

Weaver wrote this theory of translation shortly after World War II, when the computer had demonstrated great success in breaking Germany's military communication codes. In short, for Weaver, it was clear that computers were good for the tasks of decryption, and so if a problem could be reconceptualized to look like a decryption problem, then it was probably something a computer could do. Despite skepticism voiced by scientific luminaries of the day—notably Jerome Wiesner, later president of MIT and John F. Kennedy's science advisor—Weaver's "Translation" essay was enormously influential and still informs computer scientists' approaches to translation. For example, the statistical approach Weaver outlined in his essay constitutes the core of most scholarly work in contemporary machine translation.

After half a century of sustained work on Weaver's translation-as-decoding problem, how much progress has been made? When measured against the enormous amount of money that has been spent on computer programs written to "decrypt" novels, newspapers, technical reports and other sorts of texts, has the small amount of progress been worth the budgets—indeed careers—expended? Perhaps, fifty years later, it's finally time to admit Weaver's folly: translation is not a task of decryption. In fact, it may be time to critically examine many of the so-called "fixes" of ICTs with the same sort of skepticism Ludwig Wittgenstein applied in his examination of the "problems" of philosophy.[2] Many of the "problems" of computer-network-facilitated "communication" may stem from a badly chosen set of foundational propositions (e.g., translation-as-decryption) and might, therefore, be more properly understood as pseudo problems or just dangerous and silly games.

---

[1]Warren Weaver, "Translation," in W. N. Locke and A. D. Booth, eds., *Machine Translation of Languages: Fourteen Essays* (Cambridge, MA: The MIT Press, 1955), 15–23.

[2]Ludwig Wittgenstein, *The Blue and Brown Books: Preliminary Studies for the "Philosophical Investigations"* (New York: Harper & Row, 1960).

insurance

Geeta Patel

Prayer:
Back taut, smooth clothed camouflage,
Hard below a waiting dove
His body half turned towards a stupa's clarity
A soldier reaches up, lotuses cupped in his hands.
His face is framed in the flowers' luster
As though war and peace were promised in marriage.

බුදු සුවඳ දස අත පැතිරේවා

Lotus flower offered to the place where Buddha lives

Safety:
Prayers for war in the name of peace.
Prayers for life in the guise of war.
Ensuring livelihoods for a militarized nation.

Security:
Bodies divvied up into working parts.
Each part worth a particular sum.
Each part insured from the price of time spent
At labor for the state.
Death's grief paid out in compensation.

Payout:
Grief etched into my palms
I turn photographs disheveled across
A table encased in plastic.
Blood splays across the portraits of the soldier's
    broken limbs
This he tells me, is the price, the truth
He must confess for the promise
To be returned to him as cash.

The photograph is taken from a card given for the Buddha's birthday/Buddhist new year in Sri Lanka in 2001. The Sinhala on the photograph, translated by Neloufer de Mel and Robert Cruz, reads, "May the fragrance of the Buddha spread in all directions."

iRaq

Bregje van Eekelen

Forkscrew, reprinted by permission (www.forkscrew.com)

Islamic feminism

Bahíyyih Maroon

Islamic feminism emerged during the powerful second
wave of women's liberation movements during the mid-
1980s. Though a relatively recent school of thought, Islamic feminism draws heavily on the archetype of Ai-
sha, wife of the Prophet Mohammed, politician and military strategist. The political analysis of women's roles
in society provided by the work of secular nationalist
feminists such as Huda Sha'rawi and Saiza Nabarawi,
who vigorously pursued the empowerment of Egyptian
women throughout the first half of the twentieth century, have also made important contributions to contemporary Islamic feminist thought. The most powerful
current of Islamic feminism, however, pursues the advance of women's political and economic rights while
emphasizing an ongoing engagement with Islamic principles in the struggle for gender equality. Islamic feminists within this current present a marked departure
from schools of feminist thought that have previously
characterized religions of the book (Judaism, Christianity and Islam) as patriarchal structures inherently contrary to the realization of women's liberation. Utilizing theological studies, Islamic feminists have provided radical reinterpretations of canonical Muslim texts
that form the basis of *Sharia* (Muslim law). They have
recuperated previously ignored *Hadith* (sayings of the
Prophet) recorded by women in the early days of the
Umma (Muslim community), and they have actively
promoted ways of understanding Islam that enable be-
lievers in Allah to conceive of women's equality as a
constitutive element of progressive Muslim practice. Islamic Feminisms include a wide and varied spectrum
of activist reinterpretations of Islam, from the legacy

of martyrs such as Konca Kuris, murdered for espousing alternative views of Islamic practice, to the work of secular scholars such as Fatima Mernissi and Asma Barlas. The challenging voices of writers such as Irshad Manji—an observant Muslim and out-Lesbian human rights activist—continue to expand Islamic feminism.

Japan's peace constitution

Carol Gluck

Article Nine of its 1947 constitution states that Japan "forever renounces war as a sovereign right of the nation" and therefore that "land, sea, and air forces, as well as other war potential, will never be maintained." The "renunciation of war" clause, like the rest of the Japanese constitution, was written by Americans during the occupation of Japan after World War II. By contemporary constitutional standards, the provision was unique, imaginable only under conditions of utter Japanese defeat and absolute American power. Yet, the "peace constitution" established itself among a Japanese public who embraced pacifism as the primal lesson of their nation's catastrophic war.

Popular support for the "no-war clause" remained overwhelmingly strong for decades, even as the United States encouraged rearmament in a cold war context. In 1954 the Self-Defense Forces were established as a euphemism for a military force that had grown to one of the largest armies in the world by the time of its fiftieth anniversary this year. But while Japanese public opinion resisted exploding the euphemism, the U.S. government pressed Japan to spend more on defense and forsake its "free ride" on the U.S.-Japan Security Treaty. From Richard Nixon in the 1950s through John Tower in 1989, who retrospectively declared the peace consti-tution a "lousy idea," to Richard Armitage in 2001, who urged Japan to "show the flag" and support the U.S. war on terrorism, the United States did all it could to take the "peace" out of the peace constitution.

And now it seems to be working. Japan paid $13 billion in the first Gulf war in 1991, for which it received scant gratitude from the U.S. It then sent troops to sup-port UN peacekeeping operations in Cambodia and elsewhere, which seemed a big step for pacifist Japan but made little impression on its ally in Washington. So after September 11, the Japanese government respond-ed to U.S. entreaties for aid in the war in Afghanistan by passing new and sudden legislation that resulted in Japan sending warships to the Indian Ocean. It required but one further historic step for Japan to despatch Self-Defense Forces to Iraq in early 2004, breaking prece-dent with the postwar past and the peace constitution.

For the first time, more than half the Japanese peo-ple now support constitutional revision, although most do not wish to abandon the renunciation of war but rather focus on renaming the Self-Defense Force what it is: an army. But after nearly six decades of strong support for the constitution, it seems a slippery slope to move from self to collective defense, from peace-keeping operations to troops in "noncombat" zones in war-torn Iraq, and even from longtime peace to who-knows-where-or-when anytime war, as long as when the U.S. threatens and cajoles, Japan listens. Pity the poor peace constitution.

keywords industry

Hilla Dayan

The lethal keywords industry, managed by the Israeli Defense Force (IDF) and its affiliated security services, is the dominant engine of political imagination in Israel. The global proliferation of its conceptual warheads is alarming. In the IDF world where everyday life is an agglomeration of ordinary atrocities, matter-of-fact cruelties and vulgar, flagrant racisms, words have to make more than usable sense. Language is not a virus, but a Caterpillar bulldozer; it bluntly flattens, destroys, and covers up.

Lethal keywords cover our mental spaces with a dusty military blanket. Now imagine a "peace process" leading to a "better security reality."[1] What could be more conducive to freedom with "better security reality" then permanent military control? The lethal keywords industry is the source of a political imagination that fantasizes a world free from the endless chatter produced by the Israeli/Palestinian conflict. It serves well the longing for the moment tanks in refugee camps will be like doves in the blue sky. You won't read about it in the newspapers. It is therefore quite by a natural course that the "disengagement plan," *Hitnatkut* in Hebrew, was inaugurated. Try to read it aloud: hit-nat-kut. Think of the sounds it produces: Tik-Tak.[2]

Imagine a smiling fat man in a suit cutting a red ribbon.

It became necessary to replace the overdetermined concept of "Separation" to remove stains of association with the Apartheid regime ("Separate/separation"—*partition, division, disintegration, shattering, fragmentation, dismemberment, segregation, fracture, **break***). "Disengagement" however offers immediate relief

("Disengage/disengagement"—*freedom from obligation or occupation, release, get out (of), get away (from), get rid of, unite, free, **liberate***). In this light, "diet" version, disengagement is about attaining swift, painless freedom. For Israelis only.

The "unilateral disengagement plan," the "phased disengagement plan"; what is between these clean, ceremonial keywords and the total military control over the occupied territories they stand for? To further destabilize the relationship between "disengagement" and "separation," a military assault, called "a rainbow in a cloud," took place, with its memorable IDF announcement of "no situation of hunger" in the Gaza strip neighborhood of Rafah. During the assault . . . no, sorry . . . the "activity," seven people died in a "violent demonstration" (an old keyword for any number of Palestinian people gathered in protest at any time and place in the occupied territories and in Israel). Others died by the now well-known "circumstances that are still unclear," and will no doubt remain indefinitely unclarified. The missile shot at the demonstrators, was not intended to stop the protest, but—in fine military poetics—to "create an effect of explosion." All "activities" however, were necessary to destroy "the tunnels." The Hebrew word *Minharot* suggests a dark void, an immense underpass that connects one point to another. The keyword was crafted to give the impression that danger from Rafah creeps right on the doorstep of anybody's home in one of Tel Aviv's slumber suburbs, as if those ditches were exits on the "Ayalon" highway surrounding the metropolitan area.[3]

The ruckus of "a rainbow in the cloud" buried the noise of infrastructure work on the "separation wall" (also known as the "security barrier," or simply "the fence"). The building of the wall will encircle 20 square kilometers in the area east of the settlement bloc of

Ariel. "Fingernails" is the keyword for the territories confiscated from Palestinians (the "Ariel fingernail"). In the future they will mutate into full "fingers" annexing 150 square kilometers of Palestinian territories in this part alone. The Palestinian villages in between are *Muvlaot*, "cantons." Muvlaot in Hebrew comes from the same root as being swallowed up and eaten away.

Imagine a bird of prey with long claws, "fingernails," hovering, looking for something to snatch.

IDF Hebrew is used in Israel as a means of mass destruction of political imaginations. What can I say as a native speaker? Those of us actively opposed to "our" occupation look for words. We try to import, to borrow, to catch up with the daily flow of new "security talk." Some name the misery caused by it "the silent transfer," "ethnic cleansing," "apartheid," "symbolic genocide."[4] But these are mostly imported evils, not specifically "ours." They don't quite accurately capture it. Sometimes we are forced to succumb to using the industry's products, such as the diminutive, cute term "the fence," despite being horrified by the long-term implication of this monstrous barrier. It is perhaps not so surprising that our ability to produce anti-lethal keywords is so limited, that there is no available word that fits to describe the steady deterioration into something like, perhaps even worse than, anything we had known before in the history of conflicts. Imagine standing on a cliff on top of a steep abyss. The abyss grows deeper and deeper underneath you.

Imagine you can only hear the prey birds screaming.

---

[1]The disengagement plan of Prime Minister Ariel Sharon, full text, *Haaretz Daily*, May 5, 2004.

[2]Colloquially these sounds connote a quick and harmless action, like pressing a button to switch off a light.

[3]"Commander of IDF forces in the Strip: The Operation in Rafah has achieved its goals," *Haaretz Daily*, May 25, 2004.

[4]"The Silent Transfer" is used by Israeli human rights organization to describe population transfer by denying east Jerusalem Palestinians residency rights in the city. "Ethnic cleansing" and "apartheid" is in common use, mainly by activists against the occupation. Israeli sociologist Lev Greenberg recently caused a public uproar and was nearly kicked out of Ben-Gurion University for using the term "symbolic genocide" to describe Israeli practices in the occupied territories.

limbo

Margaret Brose

We are living an ironic, grotesque inversion of Dante's Inferno. Today, when expressions such as "the axis of evil" have become clichés, we need to acknowledge Hell and Limbo as present political states.

In Christian theology, Limbo designates an intermediary state or place reserved for those souls who have died and have experienced neither Christ nor the Christian Church. It was conceived expressly by the Church as the abode of the Old Testament prophets who were born before Christ, thus could not be saved, but who had committed no sin, thus should not be damned. The virtuous Old Testament souls (Adam and Eve, Moses, Rachel, Leah, Abraham and Isaac, etc.) were to wait in Limbo until Christ descended into Hell (between the crucifixion on Friday and the resurrection on Sunday) to bring them into Heaven. This doctrine was known as the "Harrowing of Hell." Limbo was also the domain of the unbaptized infants, who are born with original sin, but who had not committed any sin since they had not attained to the state of reason.

Dante Alighieri (1265–1321) provides us with the first and most powerful representation of Limbo. Dante's Limbo constitutes a radical break with preceding theological tradition, because he conceives of it as the home of the virtuous Pagans (who had been banned from Christian schemes of the afterlife, as had Muslims, because they were racially and religiously other). Before Dante, no one had speculated about the topography, physical and moral, of Limbo. Indeed, many people still assume that Limbo is a vestibule where you wait to get into Purgatory or Heaven. Not so: Limbo is in Hell, its inhabitants are eternally damned, even if their sin is one of omission. No one leaves Limbo. Dante places Limbo in a liminal zone of Hell, across the Acheron, but before the circles in which sins of commission are punished.

Limbo is the product of a binary view of salvation and damnation, a view that confidently labels its other half as evil. The present Bush administration has described the war in Iraq in similarly dichotomous terms, casting it as a religious "Harrowing," a liberation of the subaltern from captivity into freedom. Undeniably, Iraq has been transformed into Dante's Hell. Yet for people with allegiance to the founding principles of democracy, life in the United States is now Limbo. We share its disturbing psychology. Like the souls in Limbo, we remain in an eternal state of hopeless longing. Virgil, one of Limbo's inhabitants, tells Dante: "without hope we live in desire" ("sanza speme vivemo in desio," *Inferno* IV, 42). Through no fault of their own, the souls in Limbo are damned to forever desire change, but to have no hope for it. Yet, in contradistinction, our American Limbo offers the possibility, however dim, of political action. Limbo also reminds us, in a salutary mode, that sins of omission are damnable.

lip

Jennifer González

lip *Anatomy:* **a.** either of two fleshy folds that surround the opening of the mouth **b.** the margin of flesh around a wound *Slang:* insolent talk

If the insolence inherent in racist caricature proves to be among the most durable of social and semiotic forms, its wounds are equally perennial. On the receiving end of a golf club or a gun, the latest abject subject is positioned with familiar and long-standing visual tropes that proscribe the limits of political signification on the very flesh of the body. A simple drawing is all that is required to announce who the "nigger" is now.

military-industrial complex

Jonathan Beller

The Military-Industrial Complex (MIC), like its predecessor, the Oedipus Complex, has highly obvious symptoms, such as the Euro-U.S. wish to annihilate both symbolically and literally the "Others" who fathered (produced) their wealth and therefore their very beings, and less obvious symptoms, including the various constraints and limits placed on everyone's imagination by living in a global society in which "War is Peace."

Though some credit the rise of the military-industrial complex to U.S. President Lyndon B. Johnson's administration as it consolidated itself around the special interests of military contractors on the heels of a Kennedy assassination still shrouded in mystery, it would be more correct to say that the moment of the Johnson administration marks the moment when the MIC became self conscious and began to speak for itself, as it were. As early as 1947 George Orwell had already discerned a fundamental shift in the character of war. He described a world in which the two fundamental goals of science were to figure out what any individual was thinking at any given moment and to develop weapons that would kill as many people as possible in the shortest possible time. These noble goals were the necessary corollaries of a global economy in which war existed primarily to ensure the preservation of hierarchical society through the destruction of the social surplus in a psychologically satisfactory manner.[1]

As Orwell and other theorists of modernity before him pointed out, machines had the potential to liberate human beings from drudgery and therefore to render them more intelligent—too intelligent, in fact, to tolerate an elite oligarchy of exploiters. A highly literate population capable of understanding its world would quickly sweep away an unnecessary, parasitic ruling class. To preserve class structure one could easily destroy the global surplus by burying it in holes or lighting it on fire. However this would only accomplish the material preservation of hierarchical society without providing the necessary psychological justification. It is just here that perpetual warfare enters the picture, along with its material-ideological crystallization, "the military-industrial complex."

Orwell's other insight into this matter was that hereafter wars waged by nation-states were simultaneously and perhaps above all else wars on their own populations. Therefore, linked to the intensive development of weaponry were varieties of media-technologies (the televisual, the journalistic, the linguistic) designed and utilized principally for thought control and psychological organization. Even as the culture industry was (correctly) grasped by Adorno and Horkheimer as "psychoanalysis in reverse," Orwell saw it as a prosthesis of the war machine. *The national subject itself was conceived in practice as an extension of a militant state apparatus that existed to wage wars that existed to destroy wealth so that the state could continue to control populations and to wage war to destroy wealth and so on in perpetuity.* That this was an intensive, global form of rationalizing the irrational required the development of a whole new set of psychological formations to accommodate it.

Orwell himself identifies "crimestop"—the inability to understand even the simplest of truths if they go against party orthodoxy—and reminds us that stupidity is as great an achievement as intelligence and at least as difficult to attain. Other aspects include a near-spiritual affinity to empty signs such as "America" and "Freedom," an insistence that a life comprised principally of drudgery and the answering of the imperatives of survival is the highest possible attainment of civilization, the always righteous and almost unconscious reflex of radically stigmatizing differences of race, religion, geography, worldview—in short any actual difference that exceeds the officially sanctioned pseudo-differences presented as acceptable by capitalist media, and the quasi-religious self-valorization experienced by the sheer contemplation of conspicuous consumption even as the practice of it leaves the practitioner empty and cold.

This list indicates the shimmering quality of the modern-day concept of the military-industrial complex itself which seems at first glance simply to name a set of material social relations of intertwined state and corporate interests that are in the obvious if sometimes lamentable business of killing people, but also names (in a whisper) the accommodating and totalitarian psychosis of socially sanctioned mass murder, along with *an ostensibly untranscendable aesthetico-moral rubric of violence and self-destruction, and therefore an ontology and a metaphysics.*

---

[1]George Orwell, *1984* (New York: Penguin Books, 1981).

news

Bregje van Eekelen

1973 *Cape Times,* October 27: "The Minister cannot expect journalists to do violence to the English language . . . by describing guerilla warfare as terrorism at all times and in all circumstances."[1]

Baader-Meinhof (Rote Armee Fraktion), Palestine Liberation Organization (PLO), Irish Republican Army (IRA), Libya, Red Brigades (Italy), Euzkadi ta Azkatasuna (ETA), National Liberation Front (Corsica), Tupamaros (Uruguay), Naxalites (East India), Cuba, Black Panthers (USA), Students for a Democratic Society (USA), Ala Marighella (Brazil), Front de Libération du Québec, the Weathermen (USA), Revolutionary Force 9 (USA), Volunteers of America . . . One thing these groups have in common is that they have been addressed as terrorists.

Reading leftover newspaper articles on terrorism, one can piece together recurrent threads in the net that is cast over terrorism. To name a few: The desire to *name.* The desire to think of the self as a healthy body, and the other as sprawling *contagion.* The desire to change the terms of categorization: from agitators to criminals, from sabotage to terrorism, from prisoners of war to unlawful combatants. The desire to expand the legal space, so as to restrict legal rights. The desire to be vague—"any violent act." The desire to control movement. And from the fact that the following fragments of "news" are not usually brought together, I take it there is a desire to keep it fresh—the threat of terrorism needs to be new, unprecedented, growing. Covering up the wastelands of words, names, desires and tactics out of which terrorism is molded, terrorism can come about as something of the present that will be resolved in the future.

1977 "In December 1977, following an increase in bombings, kidnappings, and assassinations, particularly in West Germany and Italy, French President Valery Giscard d'Estaing called for 'European legal space' in anti-terrorist measures prior to the European Community (EC) summit conference in Dublin.

"Regarded as a serious threat to democracy, European leaders felt terrorism could become contagious unless quick, effective action was taken. In France, for example, terrorist activities had jumped from about 100 a year in the early 1970s to over 600 in 1978.

"EC governments therefore tacitly agreed to cooperate and treat terrorists as criminals rather than political agitators. Terrorism, they said, should be defined as any violent act ranging from bomb attacks, to diplomatic kidnappings, to airplane hijackings.

"But the lifting of border restrictions under original EC regulations only created later difficulties for police in their attempts to control terrorist movements across frontiers. Travelers taking automobile and train routes from West Germany to France, for example, normally only undergo perfunctory controls."[2]

1960 In the 1950s and 1960s, Cuba "eliminated the problem of hijacking by requiring body searches of all passengers and by placing armed, uniformed guards aboard planes. The guards were seated with the crews so that they could keep watchful eyes on the passengers through the peepholes set in doors which separated the crew and passenger compartments."[3]

1998 Luis Posada Carriles, a Cuban national who worked for the CIA, tells "The C.I.A. taught us everything—everything. . . . They taught us explosives, how to kill, bomb, trained us in acts of sabotage. When the Cubans were working for the C.I.A. they were called patriots. *Acciones de sabotaje* was the term they used to classify this type of operation," he added, using the Spanish for acts of sabotage. "Now they call it terrorism."[4]

What else is new(s)?

---

[1]Cited in *Oxford English Dictionary,* third edition (2004).

[2]Edward Girardet, "French Police Deal Severe Blow to Terrorists," *Christian Science Monitor,* April 3, 1980, 3.

[3]J. Mallin, *Terror and Urban Guerrillas; A Study of Tactics and Documents* (Coral Gables: University of Miami Press, 1971).

[4]Ann Louise Bardach and Larry Rohter, "A Bomber's Tale: Decades of Intrigue," *New York Times*, July 13, 1998, 10.

nightmare

Goenawan Mohamad

> I've seen a lot of patriots . . . and their patriotism was . . . bad for their prose.
>
> —*Ernest Hemingway*

After September 11, 2001, the bad prose of patriotism, notable for its lack of commas, pauses, and question marks, was everywhere in American bookstores. You would immediately come across books flaunting titles such as *What's So Great About America,* with the authors arguing that "Americans do not need to apologize for the fact that their country acts abroad in a way that is good for them."[1]

I come from Indonesia, a country where patriotism can be as expressive as anywhere else. I know there is something beautiful and powerful in being part of a larger, meaningful community. But there is always violence behind every patriotic posture, particularly in a period of hostility. It is not exactly hate. It is an impulse for exclusion.

What many Americans exclude from their patriotic moment is the memory that other parts of the world have a longer history of terrorism, where thousands of innocent people have also been killed in indiscriminate killings. Instead of rejoining the world with a shared sense of vulnerability, President Bush announced the ultimate exclusionary doctrine, "Either you are with us or you are with the terrorists."[2]

Hence, the Americanization of September 11. Not long after the tragedy, I went to New York City's Rockefeller Plaza. Before The Attack, it used to have flags of different nations adorning the small square in the center. After September 11, the Plaza authority pulled down all other flags, and in their places it hoists only the Stars and Stripes, the ubiquitous signifier of nationalism.

The American propensity is to view the problems of national security in the current "war against terrorism" as something separate from the effort to increase the institutional capacity and practical efficacy of the international legal order.

The result is a hastily built Fortress America, projecting a policy of "exception" that Carl Schmitt, the Nazi philosopher, would appreciate. The clamor of Bush's "war on terrorism" sounds like a distant echo of the opening of Schmitt's argument: "The sovereign is he who decides on the exception."[3] No doubt, it is a particularly brutal view of politics.

"Our challenge," according to Secretary of Defense Donald Rumsfeld in an article in *Foreign Affairs*, "is to defend our nation against the unknown, the uncertain, the unseen, and the unexpected."[4] The question remains whether the rest of the world is prepared to live as the *nightmare* of the United States.

A version of this essay was originally published in *Tempo*, October 14, 2002

---

[1]Dinesh D'Souza, *What's So Great About America* (Washington, D.C.: Regnery, 2002).

[2]September 20, 2001, public address.

[3]Carl Schmitt, *Political Theology: Four Chapters on the Concept of Sovereignty*, trans. George Schwab (Cambridge, MA: The MIT Press, 1985).

[4]Donald Rumsfeld, "Transforming the Military," *Foreign Affairs* 81.3 (May/June 2002).

nomads

Carla Freccero

The ghost of some sort of western civilizational thinking haunts the conflict between imperial nation-states
("city-dwellers") and something called terrorism ("nomads"). We might call it the difference between those
nation-states who make war and those others who,
from no place, make terror. Is "terrorism" an ethnos
and is it the equivalent of "nomadic"? This thought
was suggested to me by a sentence in Anthony Pagden's *European Encounters with the New World:* "Modern Europe has never quite been able to forget that the
great empires, first the Greek then the Roman . . . had
been destroyed by nomadic peoples whose capacity for
movement had made them militarily superior to civi-
lized man with his insistence on the civic benefits of
immobility."[1] François Hartog, in *The Mirror of Herodotus,* talks about how the *Histories* of Herodotus set up
an opposition between the Greeks (Athenians) as city-
dwellers and the Scythians as nomads.[2] He points out
that for Herodotus—and so for the Athenians—the
Scythians come to embody the meaning of nomadism,
and he asks what work this opposition (city-dweller/
nomad) does for the Greeks. Stephen Greenblatt writes:
"Hartog suggests that the Athenian claim to be of au-
tochthonous birth called forth the inverse fantasy: in
the Scythians, the Athenian imagination figured a people who had absolutely no attachment to any place,
who were always somewhere else. . . . For the urban
Greeks, nomadism was an indelible mark of the Scythians' distance from civility, the sign and substance of
an alien existence, the quintessence of otherness."[3]
This happens particularly at the moment war begins;
Herodotus writes: "This greatest thing they have dis-

covered is how no invader who comes against them . . . can catch them if they do not wish to be caught."[4] The indeterminacy of the Scythians/nomads is what makes them elude the grasp of the invader.

The figure of the nomad has also been used in radical thinking such as that of Gilles Deleuze and Félix Guattari in *A Thousand Plateaus*.[5] Here it is used to create an opposition between what they call the war machine and the State. The nomadic war machine is something that is outside the state and opposed to it; it is the outside that constitutes the State as State, as an inside: "The State itself has always been in a relation with an outside and is inconceivable independent of that relationship" (p. 360). The State's outside, then, would be nomadism. This might also be one way of thinking the opposition terrorist/government. But Deleuze and Guattari also apply this to a certain way of thinking creatively outside and against the State: "Every thought is already a tribe, the opposite of a State" (p. 370). They caution that nomadism does not "have an irresistible revolutionary calling" but "changes meaning drastically depending on the interactions it is part of and the concrete conditions of its exercise"; the point is more that it is an outside, a form of exteriority to the State (p. 387).

The State is that which contains and circumscribes, the nomad is that which eludes such containment and makes war on the State. If we think about nomad versus polis in these abstracted terms, then what is happening looks not like an opposition between two nations or between a nation and some specific other people, but like a containment of the nation itself, an opposition between citizen and foreigner, inside and outside. As in Athens, not all those within the boundaries of the State are citizens—it is the myth of the nation in opposition to a nomadic outside that defines us as such in the present moment; note the recent and frequent reference in the *New York Times* to "Americans" instead of people when talking not about nations but about domestic events, and the way the hijackers have repeatedly been figured this way, as mobile non-citizens, as nomads, in our midst. Such civilizational thinking on the part of the State culminates in the category of the citizen—the opposition between citizen and the foreigner—and the unsuccessful attempt to establish boundaries around the polis that will serve to distinguish it from what it is not.

Rosi Braidotti, in *Nomadic Subjects,* explains and extends Deleuze and Guattari's metaphor by suggesting that we—especially we feminists—should identify with the nomad.[6] For her, "nomadism . . . refers to a kind of critical consciousness that resists settling into socially coded modes of thought and behavior" (p. 5), and, invoking Adrienne Rich, she argues that "Nomadism is an invitation to dis-identify ourselves from the sedentary phallogocentric monologism of philosophical thinking and to start cultivating the art of disloyalty to civilization" (p. 30).

Terrorism, in its interchangeability with the concept of nomad, seems to designate a people and thus, perhaps, represents an ethnos, the fantasy-projection by a state of a group of people united by. . . what? Etienne Balibar suggests that an ethnos may be merely the arbitrary name a nation-state gives to the peoples it encloses within its borders and those it excludes, whether within or outside its boundaries.[7] If nomad versus metropolitan is, then, an old civilizational fantasy, it would seem that nomadism can *only* be the thought of the metropolitan, an imaginary and imagined space or no-place within the State. Thus, even in its liberatory deployment, the thinking of nomadism keeps us focused on the State—indeed on the empire—and keeps us firmly within the orbit of its imaginary alone.

[1] Anthony Pagden, *European Encounters with the New World: From Renaissance to Romanticism* (New Haven and London: Yale University Press, 1993), 2.

[2] François Hartog, *The Mirror of Herodotus: The Representation of the Other in the Writing of History,* trans. Janet Lloyd (Berkeley: University of California Press, 1988).

[3] Stephen Greenblatt, *Marvelous Possessions: The Wonder of the New World* (Chicago: The University of Chicago Press, 1991), 124.

[4] Greenblatt, 126–7.

[5] Gilles Deleuze and Félix Guattari, *A Thousand Plateaus: Capitalism and Schizophrenia,* trans. Brian Massumi (Minneapolis and London: University of Minnesota Press, 1987).

[6] Rosi Braidotti, *Nomadic Subjects: Embodiment and Sexual Difference in Contemporary Feminist Theory* (New York: Columbia University Press, 1994).

[7] Etienne Balibar and Immanuel Wallerstein, *Race, Nation, Class: Ambiguous Identities,* trans. Chris Turner (London and New York: Verso, 1991).

nuclear (family)

Bregje van Eekelen

On February 17, 2003, a California radio station greeted its listeners: "Welcome to life under Code Orange, day ten." To frame today's alerts, codes and colors, consider the social life of shelters, civil defense, and "alerts" in the 1950s, a time when *fear factor* was not yet a TV program. In contrast to the present, Civil Defense half a century ago worked *against* fear. The worst scenario during the nuclear arms race was helplessness sprawling, a nation falling apart in hysteria. Sociologist Guy Oakes describes three ways in which permanent war was anchored in the home of the U.S. nuclear family of the 1950s.[1] First, emotions were to be managed through participant *action,* "convincing Americans that their fears for annihilation were groundless" (p. 68). Second, *rationalization* (of amongst other things domesticity) was central: defense could be learned, implemented, routinized and improved. Third, propaganda commanded *family duty,* the responsibility of every household to defend the nation from their own doorstep. Well, not every household. A common assump-

tion was that a nuclear attack would be waged against U.S. American cities. It was agreed that cities would be sacrificed; after the radioactive dust settled, the United States would be remade from white, home-owning suburbia.

Unwilling to finance security for its citizens, the Federal Civil Defense Administration (FCDA) presented Civil Defense as a self-help matter. Families were urged to purchase and consume the safety of build-your-own shelters (after all, nuclear survival was geared toward homeowners). The family was to function as a work crew, managing their emotions through unending ac-

tion, planning, drills, progress reports, self-discipline, etc. To help suburbanites get the picture, before-and-after shots of mannequin families were aired, some well-organized and with high standards of hygiene (those who would survive), and unfortunate families whose disarray would morph to dust. Oakes casts the effects of the FCDA campaigns as follows: "Civil defense home protection recast the family as an agency of the state. When the state entered the home, patriotism, which now included nuclear housekeeping, would become a family value" (p. 72). In light of the obsessive focus on the family, one might almost forget that an attack was expected to happen during *daytime,* which made the family shelter, with most children at school, and men out of the house, a rather lonely affair.

In sharp contrast to the self-help manuals and TV spots which prepared U.S. Americans for the Cold War through detailed instructions on stockpiling supplies, food, sanitation materials, shelters, etc., it is interesting how *little* precision is currently offered in terms of instructions. While families were taught in the 1950s that nuclear fallout could be treated as dust, as something you could wipe off, wash away with a good shower, or peel off (the head of a lettuce needing to be stripped of its outer leaves), today U.S. Americans are merely told to continue their daily trips to the mall, and not much else.

Some fifty years after the home became an instrument of national security, the FCDA, which aimed to reduce private fears, mushroomed into the Homeland Security Department, an instrument to endorse public fear itself.

---

[1]Guy Oakes, "The Family under Nuclear Attack: American Civil Defense Propaganda in the 1950s," in Gary D. Rawnsley, ed., *Cold-War Propaganda in the 1950s* (London: Macmillan, 1999), 67–83.

on

Kath Weston

on a preposition designed to keep people in thrall to the things they love to think they hate. See War *on* Terror. See War *on* Poverty. See War *on* Drugs

Of course, there's also fish on rice and jam on toast, but those are the revealing exceptions that illuminate the rule. "On" subordinates as it links. "On" subordinates *you* by binding you closer to the objects of your fascination and your ostensibly renounced desires. Strawberry marmalade is the enticement, not the sliced bread. Tilapia is the headliner, not the rice. And so it is with war.

Drop the putative object of the preposition and see for yourself. What are you left with? A phrase that ushers you into the very future from which you say you want to run. War on. War on.

patriot

Carol Gluck

United **S**trengthening of **A**merica by **P**roviding **A**ppropriate **T**ools **R**equired to **I**ntercept and **O**bstruct **T**errorism is what the USA PATRIOT Act of 2001 stands for. What it means is civil liberties suspended and surveillance expanded to include the websites we surf and the library books we borrow, though they haven't yet perfected the "appropriate tools" to ascertain whether or not we've actually read them. (Not to read may be the last redoubt of civil disobedience.)

Phased **A**rray **TR**acking to **I**nterception **O**f **T**arget is one definition of the PATRIOT missile. What it provides is "advanced hit-to-kill" technology, not only for the U.S. but for the countries that have purchased it, including Israel, Saudi Arabia, and Egypt. This entirely automated but not-so-smart weapon achieved an embarrassingly low "kill rate" against Scud missiles in the first Gulf War. And in the second war in Iraq, it had what the Pentagon labeled a high "fratricide" level, meaning that it more than once succeeded in shooting down friendly aircraft. Think what the PATRIOT could do in a full-fledged missile defense system.

It's clear then: PATRIOTism is now about intercepting, obstructing, and killing. Samuel Adams—the patriot, not the beer—might have wondered what has come over us. Maybe it's time to take back the acronym. Gather the PATRIOTS: **P**eople **A**spiring **T**o **R**evolution **I**n **O**ur **T**ime pledged to **P**romise **A**ttention **T**o **R**eciprocity **I**nspiring **O**thers' **T**rust under the banner **P**eace **A**nd **T**olerance **R**eign **I**f **O**ne **T**ries. Let patriotism regain its good name in the service of honorable engagement and dissent. Patriots, act.

peace
1955

Anna Tsing

On April 18, 1955, representatives of 29 Asian and African countries convened in Bandung, Indonesia. Indonesia's President Sukarno opened the conference.

> It is a new departure in the history of the world that leaders of Asian and African peoples can meet together in their own countries to discuss and deliberate upon matters of common concern. . . . You have not gathered together in a world of peace and unity and cooperation. Great chasms yawn between nations and groups of na-

tions. Our unhappy world is torn and tortured, and the peoples of all countries walk in fear lest, through no fault of theirs, the dogs of war are unchained once again. . . . What of our newly recovered independence then?

For many generations, our peoples have been the voiceless ones in the world. We have been the unregarded, the peoples for whom decisions were made by others whose interests were paramount, the peoples who lived in poverty and humiliation. Then our nations demanded, nay fought for independence. . . .

Sisters and Brothers, how terrifically dynamic is our time! I recall that several years ago, I had occasion to make a public analysis of colonialism, and that I then drew attention to what I called the "Life-line of Imperialism." This line runs from the Straits of Gibraltar, through the Mediterranean, the Suez Canal and the Sea of Japan. For most of that enormous distance, the territories on both sides of this lifeline were colonies, the peoples were unfree, their futures mortgaged to an alien system. Along that life-line, that main artery of imperialism, there was pumped the life-blood of colonialism.

And today in this hall are gathered together the leaders of those same people. . . . Today you are representatives of free peoples, peoples of a different stature and standing in the world. . . .

And, I beg of you, do not think of colonialism only in the classic form. . . . Colonialism has also its modern dress . . . . It is a skillful and determined enemy, and it appears in many guises. It does not give up its loot easily. . . . It has been made clear that the weapons of ultimate horror will certainly be used. . . .

And do not think that the oceans and the seas will protect us. The food that we eat, the water that we drink, yes, even the very air that we breathe can be contaminated by poisons originating from thousands of miles away. And it could be that, even if we ourselves escaped hurt, the unborn generations of our children would bear on their distorted bodies the marks of our failure to control the forces which have been released on the world.

No task is more urgent than that of preserving peace. Without peace our independence means little. . . .

What can we do? The peoples of Asia and Africa wield little physical power. Even their economic strength is dispersed and slight. We cannot indulge in power politics. Diplomacy for us is not a matter of the big stick. Our statesmen, by and large, are not backed up with series and ranks of jet bombers.

What can we do? We can do much! We can inject the voice of reason into world affairs. We can mobilize all the spiritual, all the moral, all the political strength of Asia and Africa on the side of peace. Yes, we! We the peoples of Asia and Africa, 1,400,000,000 strong, far more than half the population of the world. . . . We can demonstrate to the minority of the world which lives on the other continents that we, the majority, are for peace, not for war, and that whatever strength we have will always be thrown for the side of peace.[1]

Since 1955, both peace and war have undergone many iterations. Sometimes "peace" is empty rhetoric; sometimes it covers up injustice and bludgeons us into silence. But before we give up on peace, we might consider again the Bandung mandate, and its legacy of south-south dialogue.

In 2005, Indonesia and South Africa will co-host a commemoration of the Bandung conference's fiftieth year. It is disappointing to hear how much state security dominates the official agenda.

---

[1] Sukarno, "Let a new Asia and a new Africa be born" in *Collected Documents of the Asian-African Conference* (Jakarta: Agency for Research and Development, Department of Foreign Affairs, Indonesia, 1983), 3–12.

peace
2004

Sushma Joshi

At this moment, peace, that word so glibly appropriated by all sides, feels soiled, tired, and beaten-up.

I returned home to Nepal to find an eight-year-long Maoist Peoples' War raging alongside a regime that had taken over democracy. For the last nineteen days, protests have taken place in Kathmandu against the King. Tires burn every day. The protesters throw stones from catapults and pour kerosene to ignite tires and cars. The police beat them up and break open their heads.

I click my digital camera, taking photos of my five-month-old nephew, who is growing up every moment in the midst of so many lies. My father props the newspaper by his head and coos: see, he loves to read the papers. My nephew loves TV. He twists his head back to follow the bloody faces and burning fires with an intent stare.

Both sides insist they are peaceful.

personal

Emily Jacir

photography

Martha Rosler

Photography is a bounded field of activity in which the weak imagine a special, protected dominion and the powerful have reason to feel confirmed. In this space, women—willingly or not, wittingly or not—are likely to enact the rituals of subordinate rank and deference; men strive for those of dominance and control. Within the space of the photograph, meaning is up for negotiation, but you'd never know it, since the visual field and its linguistic contextualization perpetually confirm its reputation for an essential veracity, telling truth boldly, exactly as it is—except if the image at hand is a picture of you. Photography tells us that time once existed and that space was infinite and unknowable, while simultaneously it reassures us that we have scored a piece of the action through that small rectangle—a place in a history of the world.

During war, ground-combat troops from industrialized societies, thrown out of the world of everyday life into what they term Planet Iraq (or Afghanistan, Kosovo, Somalia, . . .) to another state entirely, imagine a primitive world featuring trophies as accompaniment to ritualized bloodletting. Many soldiers, faces perhaps painted with sporty stripes and smudges, demand satisfaction from the bodies of the enemy dead. In Vietnam, some made necklaces of human ears. Some also made photos of dead, sometimes mutilated, Vietnamese, in another ritualized step. The enemy combatant (dead or captured) is feminized through submission, and the photo reconfirms simultaneously the soldier's presence on that alien, fictive planet and in real world-history. Photography functions as a powerful stand-in for modernity and home. Once made, the image trophies circulate among friends and trusted associates, and reside later on, on reentry into the "real world," under beds and in closet shoe boxes. The sight of them functions like a secret handshake in a brotherhood of the damned.

In the rapid second war against Iraq, and the longer occupation, low-ranking soldiers, we learned with a shock, routinely photographed corpses and, more often, prisoners. The photographs—each one, we were told, standing for scores, hundreds, thousands of others, some "much worse"—once made public, drove straight through the eyes into the balking consciousness of a society that simply did not want to know. Home, both as a social formation and as a wider audience of strangers, was brought to the hidden corners of prisons and interrogation chambers.

A decade earlier, in an elite-corps academy that had recently been pried open to accept women, male cadets were found with photos of a naked, crouching female cadet chained to a toilet. The woman was smiling up at the camera. This smile cannot be forced onto the faces of the Iraqi and Afghani prisoners, who had sandbag hoods placed on their heads. Sexual submission in the form of simulated sex acts was forced upon them for the purpose of the photo, now a tool in the modern torturer's arsenal—a tool aimed precisely at the males in a society in which photography of the human form is an iffy thing to begin with, and visible exposure of the naked body an intolerable humiliation. Sex, photography, humiliation . . . women.

In Iraq, the one or two women soldiers we were shown in these photos, grinning and gesturing in front of naked, hooded Arab men or holding a hapless prisoner on a dog leash, claimed that they were placed there for the photo-op by their fellow soldiers, the men. They are still wearing the smile of the female cadet chained to the toilet.

pirate—privateer— private contractor

Engseng Ho

When the King of Spain plundered the gold of America in the sixteenth century and built his invincible military, the Spanish Armada, Queen Elizabeth I got quite a fright. So she gave Sir Walter Raleigh and Sir Francis Drake hunting licenses—to hunt gold on Spanish ships. Little England became a big power giving out such licenses to hunt across the world. Those who got them were called privateers because they hunted on their

Patrick Baz/AFP/Getty Images

own private money and time—no cost to Her Majesty—and shared the prize booty with the monarch, as per contract. So *privateers* were *pirates* with licenses from their government: they were *private contractors.* And English Queens and Kings grew fat and majestic selling those foreign licenses; they listened less and less to their own people at home, and more and more to the private contractors abroad. Pirates and privateers can't be on the water forever, so they got licenses from His and Her Majesties to plunder land as well. Those were big jobs, so the private contractors pooled their money in big private corporations to get the job done. The United States of America was started by these foreign corporations, which owned Virginia, Maryland and other "plantations," private investments which became states. An ocean away, John Locke wrote the company manual for running Carolina, owned by his buddy the Earl of Shaftesbury and associates. They made up the rules themselves. Locke was company secretary, and his company manual the Constitutions of Carolina. King George III didn't own these companies, but paid for their defense. When he wanted money back, they called him a dictator, threw him out and replaced him with a constitution. No wonder he turned cuckoo.

Now they're at it again, sailing across oceans, throwing out dictators, shipping in private contractors, philosophers and constitutions. Anyone say *pirate?*

> To found a great empire for the sole purpose of raising up a people of customers, may at first sight appear a project fit only for a nation of shopkeepers. It is, however, a project altogether unfit for a nation of shopkeepers; but extremely fit for a nation *whose government is influenced* by shopkeepers. Such statesmen, and such statesmen only, are capable of fancying that they will find some advantage in employing the blood and treasure of their fellow citizens, to found and to maintain such an empire.
>
> —Adam Smith, *Wealth of Nations,* 1776, emphasis his

private

Alix Kates Shulman

What's *private?* Depends who's asking. When your government wants to find out about you, they think it's perfectly fine to investigate—secretly and sometimes forcibly—such traditionally *private* matters as the books you read, the drugs you take, the emails you send, the phone calls you make, the checks you write, the company you keep; the organizations you join, the meetings you attend, the religion you practice, your political, sexual, and medical histories—and if that doesn't give them what they want to know they may lock you up without stating the charges or allowing you counsel, take away your baby if you don't follow doctor's orders, even strip you naked and torture you in order to extract your secrets. Your *private parts* are especially vulnerable: a government, employer, or doctor may test your urine for drugs, measure your fetus for age in order to enforce your pregnancy, sterilize you without permission, arrest you as a sex worker, search your anus and vagina for contraband, condone genital mutilation, attach electrodes to your testicles, and if you have been raped or contracted HIV/AIDS, ostracize and condemn you.

But if *you* should need information from your government—from such matters traditionally considered to be of public record as who attends which government meetings, what corporations and politicians receive kickbacks and favors, what charges are lodged against you, to matters like how to use birth control or obtain an abortion, which voters were disenfranchised, or what files your government keeps on you—well then, that's *private*, don't even ask, unless you want to risk winding up on a list which can mean, if you're an organization, that you will be denied funding or have your assets frozen, or, if you're a person, that you will be outed, rendered unemployable, or perhaps find yourself deported. The public stake in knowing the extent of: global warming, pollution of air and water, HIV/AIDS and other epidemics, corporate manipulation, secret alliances, weapons of mass destruction, human rights violations (for starters) should insure that these issues stay in the public eye, but perversely governments hide, diminish, deny, and brazenly lie about them in order to keep you in the dark. You still want to know? Then sue them, and hope that the courts are not stacked against you and that the censor won't wield his blackout pen— on your record if not on you.

private contractor

see **pirate**

privateer

see **pirate**

promising

Vicente L. Rafael

To exist as a social being is, among other things, to have the capacity to make promises. "I am . . ." means before anything else "I promise to speak, to tell you something, to reveal something to you, even if it is a lie. . . ." As a performative speech act, promising is as common as it is powerful, bringing forth the very conditions which it refers to. For this reason, it arguably lies at the basis of the political and the social. The possibility of having friends and enemies hinges on the making and breaking of pledges, on bearing or renouncing obligations. Similarly, to demand and confer recognition, to address and redress injury, requires the giving and taking of testimony predicated on the promise of telling the truth—even when one commits perjury. Exchanging vows and taking oaths to forge alliances necessarily come with the risks of betrayal, hence conflict. The power of promising thus lies in forging a sense of chance and futurity, allowing for an opening to otherness. It is this possibility of promising that engenders the sense of something to come, of events yet to arrive. For when we find ourselves addressed by a promise, we are stirred by an appeal: "Believe this, believe me, even when you can't trust me, you can believe at least that you can't trust me. . . ." Promising works to the extent that we believe in the possibility of believing as embodied in covenants and contracts of all sorts. It requires a horizon of faith, without which empiricism, skepticism and cynicism would make no sense.

But promises can only be made and broken if they can be witnessed and sanctioned, confirmed and reaffirmed. They must in other words be repeatable and citable, capable of being performed again and again. Repetition underlies the making of promises, and thus the practices of politics. Technology understood as the elaboration of the technical, including the techniques of speech and writing, is then not merely an assembly of instruments for engaging in politics. It is that without which the political and the futures it claims to bring forth would simply never emerge, along with the very notion of emergence itself. Simply put, to make promises is, first and foremost, to engage in a process of making which requires tools of articulation and an aggregate of technical skills with which to operate them. Body and voice are organized and enabled by a grammar and rhetoric of gestures and speech, extended and projected by media such as print, phone, film, television, internet, etc. In other words, promising is dependent on the prostheses of techno-mediation to produce their effects on the world.

These necessarily telegraphic remarks about politics, promise and technology call for qualification. It is worth pointing out once again, as many already have, that modern technologies, especially in their globalized and militarized forms have also displaced and destroyed entire societies, placing in jeopardy the very notion of the social. Technology thus not only enables the political; it also poses a danger, precisely by threatening to put an end to the possibility of making and sustaining promises. On the one hand, technology, particularly in its telecommunicative capacity, stirs among its users a powerful sense of things to come—for example, of more expansive, more inclusive, and more rapid connections and communities. On the other hand, it can also close off possible futures by reiterating what is already known and has already been—for example, increasing alienation, economic dislocation, intensifying social inequalities—thereby vitiating the promissory basis of political practices. There can be no promising without technology. But so, too, this other possibility: with technology, there is the recurring risk of putting an end to promising, to politics and thus futurity.

punitive expedition

Mary Louise Pratt

The invasion of Iraq in 2003 was not the first time the U.S. sent thousands of troops into a desert land in pursuit of an ally turned enemy. It happened in 1916, at the height of the Mexican Revolution, and the object of the hunt was popular revolutionary leader Pancho Villa. The echoes are intriguing even though Villa had little in common with Saddam Hussein apart from his defiance of U.S. might.

On March 9, 1916, after losing the support of his former ally Woodrow Wilson, Villa attacked the border town of Columbus, New Mexico, killing seventeen U.S. citizens. Historians are still debating why he deliberately provoked the wrath of the United States, but within days General John Pershing was dispatched to the border with 10,000 troops and the fanciest new military machinery in existence. The mandate of the Punitive Expedition, as it was called, was clear: find Pancho Villa, and kill him.

By June 1916, 150,000 troops, mainly national guard, were on active duty along the border, and the script for the U.S.'s Middle East adventures was being written. Pershing's Punitive Expedition was the first war action to be accompanied by movie crews. Villa even had his own embedded reporter, the brilliant American socialist John Reed. It was the first time airplanes were used in combat (the pilots had never landed at night). It was the debut of the armored vehicle, which would evolve into the Humvees and tanks that later took over the streets of Baghdad. It was both a dress rehearsal for the machine warfare of World War I, and the last major deployment of mounted cavalry in American history.

And it was a disaster. As if practicing for Afghanistan and Iraq, the army combed the arid mountains of northern Mexico for months without laying eyes on Villa. Their huge military apparatus was a liability in the mountainous desert. The locals who were to be liberated from tyranny were strangely uncooperative and prone even to attacking their rescuers. Nobody knew the language, and who could find water for thousands of pampered American cavalry horses? Let alone gasoline for five hundred vehicles and supplies for thousands of soldiers who, like those today, expected three square meals a day? Who knew where to look if there weren't maps and every canyon (and every Mexican) looked the same? And the heat! Few of the Americans knew how to live in it. The Villistas were right at home.

However they felt about Pancho Villa, Mexicans did not welcome the American intrusion. Pershing found himself surrounded by a populace with little interest in helping him resolve their affairs. After eleven months Wilson got smart. He called Pershing (alias Bremer) home. Pershing declared victory while privately admitting he had been "outwitted and outbluffed at every turn." "When the true history of this expedition is written," Pershing recorded in a letter, "it will not be a very inspiring chapter for school children or even grown-ups to contemplate."[1] He was right. The lessons of the Pershing expedition did not make their way into the national wisdom. As of this writing Bremer has fled, but 150,000 young Americans remain behind to patrol the deserts and streets of Iraq and the mountains of Afghanistan. They should have known better.

---

[1] Paul Espinosa, "The Hunt for Pancho Villa," Public Television, San Diego (San Diego State University, 1992).

race

Mike Davis

> In an immediate and inclusive way, suspicion of the Arabs became second nature.
>
> —*Franz Fanon*[1]

Long ago a tourist in New York sent a postcard home. "If all the world became America," wrote the poet Sayyid Qutb, "it would undoubtedly be the disaster of humanity." Seconded by the Egyptian government to study U.S. educational methods, Qutb disembarked at the 42nd Street pier in autumn 1948, an admirer of liberal modernity. But he was revulsed by Truman's America and underwent a deep religious reconversion. He returned to Cairo two years later a fervent adherent of the Muslim Brotherhood and was soon arrested as its leading propagandist. After eleven years in prison, he was hung in 1966 on trumped-up charges of conspiring to overthrow Nasser. Qutb is universally acclaimed as the major philosopher of radical Islamism, if not literally, as the *New York Times* alleges, the "intellectual grandfather to Osama bin Laden and his fellow terrorists." His masterpiece, *Milestones* (1964), is routinely described as the Islamist version of Lenin's *What Is to Be Done?*[2]

Why did Qutb become the Anti-Whitman, recoiling in disgust from the legendary excitement of Manhattan? Understanding his hostility to the self-proclaimed "capital of the twentieth century" might shed some light on the genealogy of the Muslim milieux that have applauded the destruction of U.S. capitalism's most monumental symbol. Pop analysis, of course, fits the person into the prefabricated stereotype. Thus for Robert Worth and Judith Shulevitz (writing separately in the *New York Times*), the 42-year-old Egyptian literary critic and poet was, like all Muslim fanatics, a prude scandalized by big city "decadence," by the Kinsey Report, by dancing and sexual promiscuity. Indeed Qutb did complain about the "pornographic" content of much American popular culture, just as he criticized the national obsession with tending lawns to the neglect of family life and the crass materialism that smothered charity. But the great scandal of New York—and his reaction was the same as García Lorca's twenty years before—was "evil and fanatic racial discrimination." No doubt Qutb, a black man from Upper Egypt, had wounding encounters with Jim Crow.[3]

Qutb's tourist experiences today might be more traumatic. He might be in solitary confinement, without access to relatives or a lawyer, for the "terrorist" crime of having overstayed his visa or simply having aroused the suspicion of his neighbors. The real burden of the new urban fear—the part that is not hallucinatory or hyperbolized—is borne by those who fit the racial profile of white anxiety: Arab and Muslim Americans, but also anyone with an unusual head-covering, Middle Eastern passport or unpopular beliefs about Israel. For those caught squarely in the middle of this paranoid gestalt—say, a Pakistani cab driver in New York or a Sikh electronics engineer in California—there is the threat of violence, but, even more, the certainty of surveillance by powers "vast and cool and unsympathetic."[4] "Otherness"—Arabs, Korans and spores—has become the central obsession of that interminable Pentagon briefing and George W. Bush celebration that passes for American television. Indeed, the "Threat to America" (another network branding) is depicted as essentially extraterrestrial: the Middle East is the Angry Red Planet sending its monsters to live amongst us and murder us.

From "The Flames of New York," *New Left Review* 12, November–December 2001

---

[1]Franz Fanon, "Racist Fury in France" (1959), in *Toward the African Revolution*, (New York: Monthly Review Press, 1967), 163.

[2]Robert Worth, "The Deep Intellectual Roots of Islamic Terror," *New York Times*, October 13, 2001; and Anthony Shadid, *Legacy of the Prophet: Despots, Democrats, and the New Politics of Islam* (Boulder: Westview Press, 2001), 58. For a balanced assessment of Qutb's thought—a fascinating combination of anarcho-humanism and Koranic chiliasm—see Ahmad Moussali, *Moderate and Radical Islamic Fundamentalism* (Tallahassee: University Press of Florida, 1999), chapter 5.

[3]Worth, "Roots of Islamic Terror"; Judith Shulevitz, "The Close Reader: At War with the World," *New York Times Book Review*, October 21, 2001; and Shadid, *Legacy of the Prophet*, 57. See also John Calvert, "The World is an Undutiful Boy: Sayyid Qutb's American Experience," *Islam and Christian-Muslim Relations*, 11.1 (2000).

[4]H. G. Wells, *The War of the Worlds* (London: Harper & Brothers, 1898), 1.

---

real

Myra Goldberg

Sorry Ms Jackson oooo I am for real
Never meant to make your daughter cry
I apologize a trillion times

By *real,* does this amazing rapper, apologizing
    to his girlfriend's mother, mean *sincere,*
    hurtful by accident instead of design to this girl,
    who is not alone in the world,
    but is somebody's daughter.

She's *real,* an African-American woman on jury duty
    pointed to me, when I said maybe the defendant
    without an alibi hadn't robbed the victims,
    but was somewhere else that day,
    doing something else he couldn't mention
    in that courtroom.

I thought by *real,* this woman meant the story
   I'd made up to explain the boy's missing alibi
   rang true to her even if we lived
   in different neighborhoods.

Can we make up stories that will keep us *real*
   to each other? Keep us *here* from doing worse
   than is absolutely necessary to people *there.*

Is it impossible to keep it real if you have
   too much power?

What do *real* people do, my brother, in the late
   nineteen-fifties, asked my mother.

Real people were in *Life* or on TV. Not our crabby
   Jewish grandfather or the insulting Hungarian
   refugees across the street.
   Pictured people as opposed to neighbors.

If most American women wear a size twelve,
   and only pictured American women wear a size
   four, are most women unreal, or a problem
   to be solved?

Because of the slant of public discussion
   you feel *unreal* in this Rome, if you are as moved
   by a Palestinian kid shot on TV, as an Israeli kid
   bombed in a pizza parlor or some kid killed
   in NigeriaBrazilIndonesia by toxic oil contracts,
   who never appears in a picture.

"You are very courageous in your community,"
   the Palestinian woman said as we watched
   the Support Israel parade together with our signs
   against the Occupation. But I began crying
   because a people I remember as funny, ironic,

real, had become a people who feel that
only their own pain is real
and everybody else deserves what they get.

When I was a kid in the suburban fifties,
walking down a tree-shaded block,
then turning left to where there were no more trees,
I'd hear singing coming from the Ebenezer Baptist
Church that made me feel that the people inside
were real to themselves and saw the world
as big enough to hold them and other real people.
They were in there being *real* for the rest of us, I felt.

Yesterday Reverend Forbes said, "I'm not interested
in who killed Christ all those years ago.
I want to know who is killing him now."

respect

Jonathan Fox

The historic memory of Benito Juárez continues to reso-
nate powerfully among Oaxacan migrant communities.
As a result, migrant organizations took initiatives that
raised statues in his honor in prominent public places
in Los Angeles and Fresno, California, on the 197th anniversary of his birth, in March 2003. The statues' in-
corporation into the public landscapes of these cities
also symbolizes the coming of age of a new phase of
Mexican migration, one in which indigenous migrants
are taking their place in the collectively imagined Mexico outside of Mexico. Indigenous Mexican migrants' or-
ganizational initiatives and rich collective cultural practices open a window on their efforts to build new lives
in the United States while remaining who they are and
remembering where they come from. Juárez's most fa-

mous phrase bound his legacy to the principles of self-determination: "Between nations as between individuals, respect for the rights of others means peace." This message gave the two statues an unforeseen but powerful added meaning in the midst of the U.S. war in Iraq. Indeed, just two weeks before the inaugural ceremony in Fresno's main square, the migrant groups released a communiqué addressed to the presidents of both the U.S. and Mexico entitled "No to the United States' unilateral and hegemonic war!"

rewards for justice

S. Eben Kirksey

Students and soccer moms, innkeepers and employers, travel agents and teachers, factory workers and frequent travelers were all invited to join the war on terror in October 2001. A U.S. government program called Rewards for Justice then announced a competition for cash prizes of up to $25 million for anyone who could identify a terrorist. Prospective reward recipients who logged onto www.rewardsforjustice.net could hone their skills in observing and detecting terrorists. This interactive website taught hopeful competitors to recognize suspicious license plates. Teachers and students were given clues about how to increase their chances of winning the prize: "Terrorists sometimes rely on college and university libraries and databases to obtain information that can help them plan their attacks. . . . Terrorists sometimes drop in or out of specialized courses dealing with topics such as chemical compounds and formulation, aviation, law enforcement and security procedures." This program attempted to enhance U.S. surveillance capabilities. As U.S. intelligence officials experimented with digital media in the heady months after September 11, they helped create contenders for the grand prize in this game show of global war. In the words of Colin Powell: "Rewards for Justice gives us millions of additional pairs of eyes and ears to be on the lookout." Ordinary citizens have been recruited as plainclothes agents of an imperial panopticon. Over $49 million has been paid out through the Rewards for Justice program to 29 different informants.[1] These cash rewards have been given to individuals. An image of a suitcase full of cash and the caption "payments in any currency" give the impression that the money comes with no strings attached.

"Rewards for Justice gives us millions of additional pairs of eyes and ears to be on the lookout. It puts potential informants in every place a terrorist might try to hide or operate in. And it works."

Secretary of State — Colin Powell
October 10th, 2001

One definition of justice, according to the *Oxford English Dictionary,* is the "infliction of punishment, legal vengeance on an offender; capital punishment; execution." The fate of some terrorists who have been caught by the Rewards for Justice program is clear. Mir Aimal Kasi, who had killed officials at the Central Intelligence Agency, was apprehended by U.S. officials and executed on November 14, 2002.[2]

Common playground wisdom is breaking down in the war on terror. The youth of America have been taught the mantra: "Sticks and stones may break my bones but words will never hurt me." Being named as a terrorist has clear implications. A score of unfriendly men are identified as wanted terrorists on the

Rewards for Justice website. The U.S. State Department has named thirty-seven foreign terrorist organizations and Colin Powell personally intends "to choke  off their sources of financial support, and to prevent their movement across international borders."[3] The unsmiling foreigners pictured on the Rewards for Justice website are allegedly more evil than the standard strangers who offer candy to children. These bearded brown-skinned men—some who have worked in the United States as parking lot attendants, automobile mechanics, and taxi drivers—are wanted for murder and conspiracy to murder United States nationals.

Rewards for Justice is ostensibly a system for reporting on the suspicious activity of foreign strangers living in America. This system has devolved the power to name potential terrorists to anyone who has an internet connection. By participating in this panopticon, or even learning about it, hopeful competitors may themselves become subject to technologically mediated surveillance. When curious individuals browse the Rewards for Justice website, the professional cybersnoops of the anti-terror apparatus have the opportunity to begin their investigations.

---

[1] www.rewardsforjustice.net

[2] "Mir Aimal Kansi" (2004; www.rewardsforjustice.net/english/wanted_captured/Kansi.htm).

[3] "Text: Powell Identifies Foreign Terrorist Organizations" (2001; usembassy.state.gov/islamabad/wwwh01100604.html).

roads

Jeremy M. Campbell

In the summer of 1919, Lt. Col. Dwight D. Eisenhower, in what he later described as "a lark," embarked on a journey that would change the world forever.[1] It was then that Ike participated in the U.S. Army's first transcontinental motor convoy, from Washington, D.C. to San Francisco. The convoy moved mothballed equipment just back from Europe to bases throughout the interior, and took sixty-two days to make the trip. The motley array of poor roads and nonstandard bridges, slick roadways and lonely deserts without service stations conspired to halt the Army's advance on the Golden Gate, and planted in Eisenhower's mind the will to seek major improvements in how Americans exercised their freedom of movement.

During World War II the Germans succeeded in keeping (now General) Eisenhower and his troops at bay due in large part to the efficiency with which they could move guns and equipment from heartland to the fronts. In early 1945 Allied troops were able to make use of Germany's own infrastructure, however, turning the efficiency of the Autobahn network against its builders on the road to Berlin.

In 1956, Eisenhower signed the Interstate Highway Act, which called for the establishment of the "National System of Interstate and Defense Highways." The name here is crucial: constitutionally barred from influencing the business of intrastate commerce, the federal government was only able to put forth $60 billion dollars of seed money if the system were considered vital for national defense. At the dawn of the Nuclear Age, it seemed that New York was closer to Moscow's missiles than it was to Amarillo, Seattle, or even Detroit; nuclear strategy required a tighter country to defend.

The nation's newest weapon—the largest public works project in the history of the world—had a few distinguishing features. Above all else, two design criteria were emphasized: the width of interstate highways would have to be sixty feet across, including shoulders, and the right of way would have to be as straight as possible. Ensuring wide and straight roads was necessary to the freeway's role as a weapon: to move troops, tanks, and planes effectively, the network would have to extend evenly and efficiently throughout the Republic.

Building the Interstate System coincided with and enabled the largest demographic shift in U.S. history: suburbanization. Americans took to the roads like never before. The National Park system expanded. Inner cities became economic graveyards wrapped in freeways. And enough concrete and steel were poured into U.S. highway infrastructure to build one hundred cities a year.[2] At home and abroad, the freedom of the open road was retooling ecology and filling the coffers of consolidating multinational corporations.

The commission responsible for the Interstate Highway System was chaired by retired army General Lucius D. Clay, also a member of General Motors' Board of Directors. Working with Clay was Steve Bechtel, third-generation president of Bechtel Corporation.

Bechtel still builds roads—now in Afghanistan and Iraq.

---

[1]See Richard F. Weingroff, "Federal-Aid Highway Act of 1956: Creating the Interstate System" (USDOT, Federal Highway Administration website: www.fhwa.dot.gov/infrastructure/rw96e .htm).

[2]James Howard Kunstler, *Geography of Nowhere* (New York: Simon and Schuster, 1994), 78.

the rule of law

AnnJanette Rosga

"Rule of law," a friend says to me. "What does that even mean? Isn't it kind of redundant? Like saying the rule of rules or the law of laws?"

"You're right," I replied, pausing to ponder. We looked it up online, since that's apparently what U.S. government lawyers did in 2003 when they were crafting their statements of plausible deniability for torture in a Defense Department memo for Mr. Rumsfeld.

rule of law *n.* a state of order in which events conform to the law

Sure enough. According to dictionary.com it's a tautology.

"So that's how they can get away with such blatant hypocrisy," I observed to my friend. "'Rule of law' is like a double negative. It cancels itself out." Not for the first time I detected within myself a grudging admiration for this administration's versatility in language manipulation. *Crazy like a fox!*

The Department of Justice has concluded that customary international law cannot bind the Executive Branch under the Constitution, because it is not federal law. In particular, the Department of Justice has opined that "under clear Supreme Court precedent, any presidential decision in the current conflict concerning the detention and trial of al-Qaida or Taliban militia prisoners would constitute a 'controlling' Executive act that would immediately and completely override any customary international law."[1]

This Department of Defense memo, leaked to the press, is riddled with citations to dictionaries. Government attorneys are at pains to demonstrate their filial devotion to the rule of law by means of carefully cited definitions of words like "other" and "United States," and "specific" versus "general" intentions. (It is torture if the pain and suffering caused by a U.S. captor is *specifically* intended, but not if it is only *generally* intended.[2])

Not for nothing were the Republicans scandalized by Slick Willy's evasions concerning his "sexual relations with that woman." *That* president dithered on the definition of "is." ("It depends on what the meaning of 'is' is.") I see, too late, that it was indeed the dithering that bothered them. The Republicans prefer masculine certainties like these:

> Secretary Rumsfeld repeatedly has made a distinction between [applying the] Geneva Convention . . . [to] prisoners "pursuant to those rules or consistent [with] those rules" and he said . . . a few days ago, that the Geneva Convention did not apply "precisely" [to the treatment of prisoners in Iraq].[3]

Stirring glissandos invite us to swoon with patriotic fervor and self-righteous calls to arm ourselves and (selected) others:

> In Iran, the desire for **freedom** is stirring.
> In the face of harsh repression,
> Iranians are **courageously** speaking out
> for **democracy**
> and **the rule of law**
> and **human rights.**
> . . . By replacing corruption
> and self-dealing, with **free markets**
> and **fair laws,**
> the people of the Middle East will grow in **prosperity**
> and **freedom.**[4]

By such simple means are we encouraged to forget that the law has only ever been what those with power interpret it to be.

Arendt's study of the Nazi bureaucrat Eichmann shows us that the moral and ethical standards of a society can be upended by the simple process of imposing new rules. "Eichmann had always acted according to the [strict] limits allowed by the laws and ordinances . . . [as did] a bureaucratic . . . mass of men who were perfectly normal, but whose acts were monstrous."[5]

"Rule of law," a friend says to me. "What does that even mean?"

"I don't know," I reply. "Maybe it just means there's a paper trail."

[1]Department of Defense Draft Memo "Working Group Report on Detainee Interrogations in the Global War on Terrorism: Assessment of Legal, Historical, Policy, and Operational Considerations (March 6, 2003)," 6. The memo can be viewed at www.npr .org/documents/dojmemo30020306.pdf.

[2]"The 'Torture Statute' (18 U.S.C. sec. 2340) requires that a defendant act with the specific intent to inflict severe pain. . . . [However, if] the defendant acted knowing that severe pain or suffering was reasonably likely to result from his actions, but no more, he would have acted only with general intent'" and would not therefore be guilty of torture (Department of Defense Memo, 8).

[3]From questions by Senator Senator Carl Levin, Democrat from Michigan, to Undersecretary of Defense for Intelligence Cambone, in: Kirk Semple, "General Blames Command and Training Lapses for Prison Abuse," New York Times, May 11, 2004 (www.nytimes .com/2004/05/11/international/middleeast/11CND-ABUS.html ?ex = 1088740800&en = af3eeb697cc42c96&ei = 5070&hp).

[4]Remarks by President George W. Bush in Commencement Address at the University of South Carolina, Columbia, May 9, 2003. Office of the Press Secretary (www.whitehouse.gov/news/ releases/2003/05/20030509-11.html).

[5]Bethania Assy, "Eichmann, the Banality of Evil, and Thinking in Arendt's Thought," paper given at the Twentieth World Congress of Philosophy, Boston, Massachusetts (August 10–15, 1998; www.bu.edu/wcp/Papers/Cont/ContAssy.htm).

security

Mary Louise Pratt

Security is one of those words, like "celibacy" or "short" that invokes its opposite. As soon as you mention security, you suggest there's a danger, or a potential danger. Otherwise the subject wouldn't be coming up. So talking about security is one of the most effective ways to cause fear. It's effective because you're not talking about fear, you're assuming it's there—or should be. If somebody starts talking about your security, to make sense of what they're saying you have to identify with being afraid, assume you *should be* afraid. If you're not, you're increasing the danger even more by being an idiot or a feckless naïf.

Security language revolves around particular kinds of dangers. It's about enemies and violence. Its operative measures involve barriers, locks and guards. You secure borders by building security fences; you elaborate security gates at airports; you screen people's luggage or their eyeballs. When the dangers are internal and known, we talk about safety, not security. Safety is something we can collectively create for ourselves. The response to HIV/AIDS was safe (not secure) sex. Reducing speed limits increased highway safety, not highway security. Workplace safety is about wearing hardhats and limiting overtime. Home safety means putting kiddie locks on cupboard doors and skid mats in showers. Home security means battening the hatches against potential intruders.

Because security is about enemies and the unknown, it can be hard, when someone comes along wanting to guarantee your security, to say "Thanks anyway." But you're not afraid, you really don't see that you're in any greater than everyday danger, you don't see the need for what it is that they want to do on your behalf, nothing in your own knowledge and experience indicates the need for changes. You could be wrong. The dangers are unknown. If you *are* wrong, once you've declined to be afraid, whatever happens to you is your own fault. Before you were just living. Now you're living at your own risk. *Your own risk.* Declining security also puts you in disagreement with the person with the power to offer it to you. That in itself can be dangerous. After all, the authorities who guarantee your security (as opposed to your safety) are the ones who have, as the theory says, a monopoly on the legitimate use of force.

Women and girls know plenty about this. We're told all the time to stay indoors, never go anywhere alone, etc., by beneficent forces that at the same time encourage us to perform femininity in myriad ways that endanger our health and well-being. Even as we've empowered ourselves to decline these things, we're told that we do so at our own risk, and when bad things happen it's our own fault.

What creates safety and well-being aren't actions against enemies, but measures that keep relations of enmity from arising, or from erupting into violence when they do. If there are going to be borders you need all kinds of relationships across them so that surprise crises don't happen. You need to cultivate and value people with the knowledge to maintain those relationships and shape them. We are safer in peace, not war. Everybody knows that.

seeking heroes

P. A. Ebron

shame

Iain Boal

If "shock and awe"—euphemism (with religious over-tones) for old-fashioned *Blitzkrieg*—indelibly conjures the invasion of Iraq, "shame" is the symptom of its occu-pation. In the spring of 2004 the imperial psyche found in Abu Ghraib its savage feast, and in a text by Rapha-el Patai entitled *The Arab Mind* it apparently found its catechism. Originally published in the early seventies, though actually belonging to an earlier World-War-II genre of "national character" studies and anthropology-at-a-distance, Edward Said had cited it as the very epit-ome of crude orientalism. It was reprinted in time for the invasion and became, according to Seymour Hersh, "the bible of the neo-cons in Arab behavior," as well as a war college handbook on humiliation—in particular the chapter on "sex as a taboo vested with shame and repression," where we are informed *inter alia* of "the Arab view that masturbation is far more shameful that visiting prostitutes."[1]

Hersh's report helped to explain the source of so much talk of Muslim shame and sexuality, suddenly on the lips of pundits all over the licensed media. So now we know why Arabs—unlike, say, Anglo-Saxons—find being stripped naked in front of attack dogs and grinning torturers especially disturbing and shameful. Muslims, we must understand, inhabit shame-cultures, shame being more primitive than guilt, which is Judeo-Christian, enlightened, modern. And, of course, we already have it on Erik Erikson's authority that, psychologically, guilt is a more "advanced" emotion than shame. Torture chambers and safehouses—those spaces of shame—litter the hinterland of the base world of the American empire. The names Abu Ghraib and Guantánamo now stand for a gulag that encompasses the planet. Still, it should be remembered that one quarter of all the world's prisoners are inside the United States, and they also know plenty about humiliation, sexual and otherwise. Shame on us.

---

[1]Seymour Hersh, "Chain of Command," *The New Yorker* (May 17, 2004), 38–43; Raphael Patai, *The Arab Mind* (New York: Hatherleigh Press, 2002), 144.

shave

see **beard**

sick

see **chicken**

speech

Sharon Hayes

When George W. Bush addresses me, the "people of the United States," I think of theater. I am not speaking of theater as metaphor but rather strategy.

Bush is not the scripted, acted character of a President because he is not capable of being a "real" President. He is the character of our President because the tasks of the actor are useful: observe the invisibly potent fourth wall, maintain one reality, block out all noise, disruption, or input from the audience and speak, speak, speak. The strategy of disagreeing with or contradicting the scripts constructed by the Bush administration is doomed to a battle of tenacity and repetition. In such struggle, we will never wholly lose the space of the collective imaginary but neither will we manage the harder task, to disrupt and refuse this "war." If our presence as listeners, as fictive as it may be, is necessary to the event of Bush speech, how can we actively not show up to fulfill this role? If we are an audience who actively refuses to receive that thing that George W. Bush does when he opens his mouth, can it still be called speech?

stomach

Donna Hunter

Every day but one since the start of the war in Iraq coffins leave the Middle East, on a flight to Dover Air Force Base (Dover, Delaware), the site of the largest military morgue in the world. By late May 2004 the remains of more than 700 members of the U.S. armed forces had arrived at this Air Force base. At the time of the first war in Iraq (1991), the first President Bush imposed a ban on images of the war dead arriving at Dover (and, it appears, on any formal ceremonies at the base). He supposedly took extreme umbrage when he was shown on television making a statement about the war while the other half of the screen showed coffins arriving, each draped in an American flag. (Some bloggers maintain that Bush was shown playing golf.) The first Iraq war is also the moment that references to "body bags" were replaced in military parlance by references to "transfer cases," reusable aluminum containers for transporting body bags. A case is less abject than a bag, especially one with a dead body in it.

The Department of Defense has said that the ban was introduced and is maintained out of respect for the dead and their loved ones: it protects their right to privacy; it preserves dignity; it prevents "unwarranted attention." But there are other reasons, as the military knows. In January 2000 then-Chairman of the Joint Chiefs of Staff General Hugh Shelton said that American deaths in any future war would have to pass the "Dover Test": how many coffins can the American people stomach seeing before turning against a war? The abject again: how many can we stomach?

In November 2003 a self-styled "media archeologist" (Russ Kick) filed a Freedom of Information Act request for the release of any photographs of coffins at Dover AFB. His request was refused; he appealed. At the end of April 2004 he unexpectedly, and mistakenly, received a CD with 361 images. He immediately posted them on his web site (thememoryhole.org).

We know there is a "right to see," or should be, protected by the First Amendment. Seeing can be believing: seen one by one, the transfer cases represent each ineluctable death, a death each viewer can imagine as her or his own or that of a loved one. The aggregate number of war dead, a number given daily in newspapers and on the nightly news, is better understood when one counts, like a child, one flag-draped body (or the "re-associated" portions of a body) after another.

Three days before the second war in Iraq began, a speech that General "Blood and Guts" Patton gave to American troops in England the day before D-Day was posted on freerepublic.com, "A Conservative News Forum":

> War is a bloody, killing business. You've got to spill their blood, or they will spill yours! Rip them up the belly. Shoot them in the guts. When shells are hitting all around you and you wipe the dirt off your face and realize that instead of dirt it's the blood and guts of what once was your best friend beside you, you'll know what to do!

Several of those who responded to the posting only wished that the United States had such a military leader as the country stood on the brink of another war. In 1944 the wrenching of guts was the impetus to act heroically; in 2003 it was to be avoided at all costs.

streamline

James C. Scott

Imagine you are a U.S. state governor or a corporate CEO who wants to slash spending, fire employees, close branches or plants, and avoid pension obligations. How can you put it across; how can you minimize the "turbulence"; how can you sugar-coat this bitter pill? It will help if you call it "streamlining." Enter the reassuring image of a sleek, smooth, efficient organization slicing effortlessly through dangerous straits.

"Streamlining" is a textbook example of what might be called a widely traveled, high-modernist euphemism. Originally, it had a quite specific, measurable meaning in fluid and aero-dynamics. Because it also carried with it the apparent authority of modern science, progress and efficiency, it became a portmanteau—a legitimating module—that was torn from its moorings in applied science and redeployed in settings where it made no scientific sense whatever. It did, and does, however, make abundant ideological sense both as a legitimating disguise and a comforting form of self-hypnosis for troubled executives.

Consider the term's wayward path from science to ideological disguise. The "streamline" in its strict sense is the tracing or representation of the flow of a fluid (e.g. water, air) past a body/object designed to minimize friction or resistance. "Streamlines" were described, theoretically, as early as the mid-eighteenth century but only photographed much later by the use of smoke in wing-tunnel tests. Non-streamlined bodies created turbulence and eddies, which, as partial vacuums, increased drag—and hence reduced speed and efficiency. The basic streamlined shape resembles an ultra-smooth horizontal teardrop, blunter at the leading (upstream, upwind) edge and tapering evenly to a sharp point at the trailing edge. Airplane wings, ship hulls, dirigible shapes, submarine forms, not to mention birds wings and fish, approximated this form and smoothness as does the latest gear in bicycle racing, skiing, and swimming.

The romance of the airplane, its place as an emblem of speed, power, distance, and modernity itself, goes a long way toward explaining why "streamlining" traveled so far and so successfully. If, as the visionary architect and designer Norman Bel Geddes declared in 1932, "Speed is the cry of our era," then, "streamlining was its metaphor and 'look.'"[1] Streamlining, in its vulgar form, took over the aesthetics of design and advertising for the automobile. Cars quickly acquired swooping backs, teardrop fenders, chrome "speed-whiskers," and shiny curved surfaces. Some of this actually reduced wind resistance but most of it, as later with fins, "portholes" and rocket- or torpedo-like prows, was entirely visual: the modern "streamlined look." The Chrysler and DeSoto "Airflow" series, "Airstream" trailers, "Zephyr" and "Bullet" trains cashed in on the romance of streamlining.

Thousands of objects that never moved were given the streamlined "look." Toasters, vacuum cleaners, cigarette lighters, lamps, teapots, pitchers, cameras, refrigerators (!), pens, chairs, desks, movie theaters, hotels, gas stations, women's dresses were "streamlined" even if it only meant rounded, smooth, shiny, vaguely teardrop shapes because it meant "modern" and it sold. In painting and sculpture, from the Precisionists—Sheeler, Demuth, and Stella—to Brancusi's birds and fish, the look of rhythmic lines, simplification of form, and elimination of detail prevailed.

Nearly a hundred years old, even in its aeronautical sense, "streamline" has not lost its magic in this postmodern world. Try "Googling" it. The mind boggles at its power and promiscuity: "streamline your life," "streamline your body," "streamline accounting," "streamlined computing," "streamlined placement," "streamlined marketing," "streamlined distribution," "streamlined taxi service," "streamlined budgets," "streamlined application processes," "streamlined mortgages," "streamlined oil refinery construction." It's become just a synonym for lean, fast, efficient. That would be merely amusing, so long as we overlooked the insult to the careful use of language.

But the real political value of the term is as an "anti-politics machine." It functions, like "development" and "efficiency" which also carry a powerful ideological charge from modernism, to throw sand in the eyes of the public, to convince them that neutral experts are selecting the best possible means to achieve ends on which we would all agree. Thus: "AOL slashes jobs to streamline operation"; "Medicare claims and eligibility to be streamlined." There's no politics here, folks: no moral choices, no hidden agendas. "Streamlining" is just a matter of technical planning and rational choice. If you know what's good for you, you won't peek behind the curtain. That's what they hope anyway.

---

[1]Richard Guy Wilson, *The Machine Age in America* (New York: Brooklyn Museum in association with Abrams, 1986), 125.

television

Vicente L. Rafael

From Monday to Friday between 5 and 6 pm, a minor miracle takes place at my home in Seattle. The tabloid show, "TV Patrol" is broadcast via satellite and cable from Manila to my part of the Pacific Northwest in the U.S. The image of well-known personality Corina Sanchez suddenly appears on my television set, the sound of her voice filling the room, bringing stories and images of current events in the Philippines. This is in some ways nothing short of miraculous. That which is distant instantaneously comes close, and that which is absent magically becomes present. Yet, the proximity of this distance does not result in dissolving the great gulf that separates me from the Philippines, but rather further amplifies it. And the presence of images and voices does not bring to my home what they represent—for example, the faces of politicians, the streets of the city, the suspected thief apprehended by the police. Instead, they keep such people and things at bay.

Thanks to the medium of television and the mediation of "TV Patrol," the Philippines is there by not being there. It thus comes to me as a kind of spectral nation. Whenever I turn on the television, I welcome without always intending to and without comprehending how, these ghosts, the spirits of the nation emanating from my original home into my present one. In doing so, I take for granted the largely mysterious because unseen processes that make such transmissions possible: the satellite feeds, the computer software and electric impulses that carry waves of sound and bits of visual data, as well as the tangled political economy of private ownership, government regulation and media conglomerates and so forth. I cannot see what enables me to see: the invisible and secret operations, the arcane codes, the endless calculations that power the transmission of this spectral nation.

them

Lisbeth Haas

Unlike *it,* which can be a subject and yet carries little emotional impact, *them* remains a grammatical object, and yet invokes the strongest of emotions. Though an object without history, *them* exerts substantial influence on people's thoughts, generally conveying damning attitudes towards those referred to. A film produced about *Them!* (1954) places science and the military against Them: the Ants, the Female Reds. As today, the struggle against Them involved the cold war (now transmuted) and the ongoing gender war. *Them* remains an ephemeral category of people who exist and change in relationship to the highly mutable "us." (See **us** for further detail.) The Dictionary of Local and International Solidarity suggests that one avoid the accusatory undertone associated with Them by changing the emphasis in pronunciation to TheM, drawing out the mmmmmmm thereby making the implied difference sound quite delicious. Emphasizing mmmmmmm wherever appropriate. It's best to probe the who behind them, especially when in large crowds.

time

Morgen J. Lennox

"A man whose time is money to him must attend not only to his hours and minutes, but even to his seconds," wrote an editor for the *New York Times* in 1877.[1] This equation of profit and duration came to make sense through the standardization of time.

Before the railroad industry became involved in

standardizing time, the effort towards uniformity had been dominated by a tiny group of scientists. In the 1840s, British railway companies each created their separate and competitive standards of time. By 1848 the London and Manchester Railroad had won the fight of petitioning parliament to accept London or Greenwich time as that of the nation.[2] Many communities around the world still preferred, however, to offer their own standards of time, including "God's time."

Opposition existed against the standardization of time in the United States, with workers and independent towns opposing the dominance of the railroad companies. Yet once the U.S. federal government had won the battle for standardized time at home, it was ready to impose the system on the world. In 1884, the U.S. government organized an international conference to standardize time around the world for science, for commerce, for the "national interests" of Great Britain and the United States, and, of course, for the "common good of mankind."[3] Of the twenty-five countries represented at the conference, only France objected, but unsuccessfully. Perhaps such imperial highhandedness sounds familiar.

Colonialism spread imperial time to places such as India, where people learned to count time by the passing of the British-sponsored railroads. Triloki Pandey recalls that when the train passed his village, it was time to get up and start working. The train, he joked, had replaced the rooster. Yet colonial time did not take over all time; alternatives continued to flourish alongside standard time. Muslims around the world, for example, have continued to measure time by direct solar and lunar measurements, as agreed upon by regional religious authorities. Yet Muslims cannot ignore imperial time. In many areas, Muslims contrast "local time" and "official time," pitting community affiliation against the state, and religion against imperial standards. Even in 1979, Ruhollah Mousavi Khomeini, the Ayatollah and religious leader of Iran, complained, "The heads of our countries are so influenced by the West that they have set their clocks according to European time. It's a nightmare."[4]

[1]William Peirce Randel, "They Didn't Know What Time It Was," *American Heritage* 34 (October/November 1983), 103.

[2]Alasdair Nairn, *Engines That Move Markets* (Canada: John Wiley & Sons, 2002), 6.

[3]Eviatar Zerubavel, "The Standardization of Time: A Sociohistorical Perspective," *The American Journal of Sociology* 88.1 (July 1982), 14.

[4]Zerabuvel, 19.

tough questioning

Ben Carson

When the U.S. military openly violates aspects of the Geneva Conventions in Iraq, national media culture maintains an eerie tone of legitimation. The frame of controversy, if any, has almost never involved questions of whether (and how) an ongoing, widespread, and grave horror, with no obvious purpose in sight, can be stopped. Rather, journalists have concentrated on issues of how much war crime is politically acceptable, and under what vague circumstances. This exercise has been a piteous abuse of words and reasoning.

The problem is evident even in vocabulary. In an interview with WAPV Jackson, Mississippi ("Lott: Tough Questioning OK if Lives Saved"; AP, May 27, 2004) Trent Lott encourages prolonged humiliation, fear of electrocution, and physical intimidation, as important methods of interrogating Iraqi and Afghan civilians. "[The] physical perversion is inappropriate . . ." he explained to the television crew, regarding photos of men being humiliated and terrorized at Abu Ghraib prison. "But . . . this is a very tough situation. You have got to have sleep deprivation, you have got to scare them, you have got to threaten them." Such techniques are what is meant by the headline words "Tough Questioning," and by the word "abuse" elsewhere in the article.

I really don't understand this terminology. "Tough questioning" means illuminating unusual problems, or challenging assumptions about something. I *like* tough questioning. Tough questioning is *always* OK, even if lives aren't saved.

We have a word for it when you hold a vicious dog close to the face of a tied-up naked human being. We have a word for it when, in systematic fashion, you deprive people of warmth and sleep, and then shout insults and false indictments at them. When writing about deliberate and controlled violence, inflicted on people being held captive, the proper word is *torture.* No thesaurus, please. The institution of objective journalism has only one word available for this stuff—*torture* describes, and certainly understates, what we now know to be pervasive in this miserably sad war . . . what Lott says is "inappropriate," as well as what he casually advocates.

The dispassionate headline should be "Lott Advocates Torturing Innocent Prisoners." Yes, just to confirm: the photographed victims were *innocent,* in the familiar sense of "until proven guilty." Which is not to mention that 90 percent of them were probably (even according to the dispassionate headlines) "arrested by *mistake.*" (See "Red Cross: Treatment of Iraqis . . ." CNN, May 10, 2004.) And now here's more confusion— why does the crucial word "innocent" get left out, while the word "mistake," suggesting innocence, gets added in where it clearly doesn't belong?

trauma

Joseph Dumit

> If they don't get treatment, sometimes they never get over it.
>
> —"Post-Trauma Stress Looms," *Newsday*, September 13, 2001

The popular war on terrorism is being medicalized. Americans are trying to "get over" what is still going on. Every day there are articles in the newspaper teaching us that the "profound sadness, recurring nightmares, hyper-alertness, horror, edginess, anger, numbness" we experience are symptoms. The risk for many of us, we are told, is that our "normal reaction to abnormal events" will turn into a full-blown disease. Our feelings are to be identified as symptoms in order to diagnose an increasing variety of syndromes that may result from the traumatic event. Depression, panic disorder, PTSD are all threats. If this is the case, many of us will not "recover" from our traumatic symptoms, but instead spiral down into a syndrome.

The feelings people have of profound sadness, so deep we seem numb, even if we have only witnessed the events on TV—this feeling is compassion, a word meaning "sharing pain." These feelings have us reach into our souls to share the pain of those who are unconscionably killed, tortured, and traumatized. The very same compassion that seemed so distant to U.S. Americans when we watched cities being bombed on TV in other countries before September 11 is now activated by that same TV because now it is "us" that has been devastated.

The anger, resentment, vengeance, even hatred we feel toward unknown enemies—these are desires for peace. We are bloody angry that we can no longer sleep soundly at night; we are vengeful against all who participate in violent attacks on normal people. We want this violence, this disruption, and this horror to stop now and in the future. Peace does not mean an abdication of responsibility. Desire for peace is a primal, forceful emotion, an insistence that the world is not right and needs to be changed.

Experts tell us the opposite: these feelings are not political at all. They are not even conscious, but simply bodily, neurochemical reactions to horror. We, cultural and symbolic beings, are affected by this interpretation. It is a terrifying reframing of our lives: in the face of our bodily selves crying out to the world in solidarity and compassion, we are told: "Wait, and the symptoms will pass." If they don't, there are treatments. Treatments so that you will be numb to your numbness, so you will no longer be angry at your anger, so you will be happy in your distance, so you will be able to work without thinking of your fears.

The psychiatric approach to political trauma is to make it each individual's problem. If you are shaken up for a few days and then are able to go back to work, you are normal. If not, you are the problem. This is so twisted it is scary. It should scare you. These feelings are social, not individual; they are political, not medical. Just because you are able to bottle up all of those feelings of solidarity and compassion and go back to the way you lived and worked before September 11 doesn't mean you are normal. It means you have achieved denial.

type

Courtney L. Fitzpatrick

type *v.* to classify according to a particular system

From Daguerreotype to Genotype

We crave the orderly pattern produced by the connectedness of *things a* (cause) to *things b* (effect). We are eager to be seduced and tricked, for even just a second, into believing (un)believable lies. Science is mined for nuggets that appeal to this tendency and the growing body of genomic sciences has been a fertile plot. The genetic code is repeatedly stripped of its inherent connectedness to the organism that it represents. It is pinned to the wall and lauded as the newest screen on which we can project our recurrent fantasy: that we can classify and order life once and for all.

Students of biology now are extracting DNA from organisms (blood, tissue, dung), amplifying (copying) it in polymerase chain reactions, and analyzing results of genetic data in dizzying numbers. A world without genetic analysis will soon be as unthinkable as a world without photographic images. Like genomic sciences that now hold the intoxicating promise of control, the photograph has also occupied this role in the collective imagination. We have tried through photography to keep (youth, loved ones, memory), to systematize (the poor, the mentally ill, the hysterical, the criminal). To control. The photograph has lent itself to this practice because of its inherent connection to *what has been.* Roland Barthes writes, "every photograph is a certificate of presence" (p. 87).[1] Like the camera, the PCR machine certifies an actual presence, is the site in which the real becomes the referent, and the copied stretches of DNA are, like the photograph, a literal trace of that referent, the organism, touching us "like the delayed rays of a star" (p. 81).

Like the photograph, the genotype feeds into our fantasies of control. It can be employed in campaigns to keep us afraid (disease and clones), as photographs are employed to keep us afraid (criminals and the "Third World"). *But they both also persistently refuse.* The photograph will always already speak to the life (and death) of the referent. The genotype will always be married to the life of its organism, its environment and population. Barthes again: "The photograph belongs to that class of laminated objects whose two leaves cannot be separated without destroying them both" (p. 6).

Like the photograph, the gene and the life of its organism cannot be separated without destroying them both. Genomics are invoked by imperialist powers and popular discourse to perpetuate our (mis)understandings of causality (gene a → trait b), to strengthen our temptations to believe in the possibility of *final* control. Yet the gene, a priori, like the photograph, will also demand loyalty from us to our own ability to resist.

---

[1]Roland Barthes, *Camera Lucida; Reflections on Photography* (New York: Hill and Wang, 1981).

us

Neferti Tadiar

us (also **U$**) first person familiar pronoun of United States of America (**US**), short for Uncle Sam, the objective case of we, Americans (also, we, the world) [origin late twentieth century, popular usage early twenty-first century]

1 a: an incontestable moral choice in a global crusade, equivalent to good in the choice between good and evil ["Either you are for us or you are with the terrorists"]
—*George W. Bush (U.S. Caesar), September 20, 2001*

b: a war cry used to demand transnational allegiance to the political-military aims and attitudes of a U.S. state-corporate power merger realized through the preemptive "war on terror"

c: those who are willing (as in "coalition of the willing"), that is, who consent to or choose not to resist the massive human, social and environmental destruction inflicted on peoples and places mythically regarded as the source of violence, a destruction inflicted in the name of moral right (see **1a**), also known as freedom (as in "operation freedom")

2 a: patriotic citizen of an imperial nation tacitly understood to have an ideal political and social system characterized by the rule of wealth, racial privilege, private property, state sovereignty and military might

b: bearer of civilizational democracy, bearer of the post-globalization white man's burden, borne on behalf of religiously and racially degenerate populations unfit for self-governance

c: an imaginary people whose defining boundaries are demarcated by *them* (marauding Third World barbarians or, often indistinguishably, terrorists, see **them**), characterized by self-evident value, superior human properties and capital virtue (signified by $)

d: members of a gated humanity

3 a: the state or condition of righteousness and blessedness, interchangeable with America [God bless America, popular U.S. incantation, insignia on U$ currency]; ["In all that lies before us, may God grant us wisdom, and may He watch over the United States of America"—George W. Bush], the embodiment of goodness, worth, merit (opposed to moral depravity, wickedness, lack)

b: a people considered vulnerable to violence because desireable, possessor of undeniable social virtues, rights and privileges, the envied fortunate, used as direct object of others' reprehensible actions and illegitimate desires ["Americans are asking, why do they hate us? . . . They hate our freedoms— our freedom of religion, our freedom of speech, our freedom to vote and assemble and disagree with each other"]

—George W. Bush, Address to a Joint Session of Congress and the American People, September 20, 2001

I WANT YOU
FOR U.S. ARMY
NEAREST RECRUITING STATION

Etymology: 1916, as U.S. enters World War I: publication of famous recruitment poster of Uncle Sam with finger pointed to the viewer and the words "I want YOU for U.S. Army" written underneath, is printed. How "you" became "us" is the history of the rise of the U$ and the consolidation of a citizenry fully identified with the imperial state.

4 us and them: *chiefly critical or ironic.* used in dissenting speech to indicate ideological work in the service of social antagonism and war and to suggest the potential ways we might think our "we" differently ["Us and them /And after all we're only ordinary men / Me and you / God only knows it's not what we would choose to do"]; a symbolic weapon that operates in tandem with the usual instruments of war ["Haven't you heard it's a battle of words / The poster bearer cried / Listen son, said the man with the gun / There's room for you inside"]: used to underscore the stakes in the deployment of the word ["Down and out / It can't be helped but there's a lot of it about / With, without / And who'll deny it's what the fighting's all about"

—Pink Floyd, British Band, "Us and Them," 1973]

vertically integrated

Jonathan Fox

Though the Nahua represent the largest indigenous group in Mexico, and some have been coming for many years, their migrants have not sustained visible membership organizations in the United States. Yet this does not mean that they are not organized or capable of cross-border collective action. On the contrary, it turns out that Nahua transnational communities from the state of Guerrero carried out a pioneering and highly successful public interest advocacy campaign in defense of their villages against a planned hydroelectric dam in 1991. The project threatened to displace an estimated 40,000 people in the Alto Balsas valley, damage a critical ecosystem and flood a major new archaeological site. Local communities drew on existing cross-village social ties and local marketing networks to quickly build a highly unified and cohesive regional movement, gaining national and international leverage in the context of the pending 500-year anniversary of the Conquest. Migrants not only contributed funds, drawing on their traditional quota system for village fiestas; they were involved in campaign strategy and tactics as well. Migrants brought video cameras to tape the movement's mass direct actions in a state known for intense repression. This tactic not only served to inform *paisanos* in the U.S., it also pioneered what became the Mexican indigenous movement's now widespread use of video to deter police violence. Migrant protests in California also drew the attention of Spanish-language television, which led to the first TV coverage of the Alto Balsas movement within Mexico itself. Their combination of region-wide, national-level and transnational organizing, crosscut by multi-sectoral alliances with environmentalists, anthropologists and human rights activists, pioneered what could be called a "vertically integrated" approach to public interest campaigns.

video

Maple Razsa

In a former Yugoslav army base only 100 meters from what is now the Hungarian-Slovene border, local activists organized their second Noborder Camp in August 2002. On the last night of the camp many express frustration that we have not taken more radical action against the nearby European-Union-funded immigrant detention centers. When we visited the centers earlier in the week we had seen desperation in the eyes of those gathered in this unlikely place: Cubans, Iraqis, Chinese, Afghans, Roma, and Serbs.

That last night we watch a video shot in the remotest desert of Australia where a Noborder Camp (www.woomera2002.antimedia.net) had been held at the Woomera Detention Center. The Noborder Camps had by then become a globally popular tactic: protest camps at the borders, detention centers, airports and even information hubs of the global migration regime, with a common demand for a freedom of movement for humans to match that developed for goods, services and capital over the past twenty years (see www. noborder.org). At Woomera some 1500 protesters converged to protest the draconian immigration policies of the Conservative Howard government. The video, *Holiday Camp,* contains powerful documentary images. When the hundreds of inmates inside learn that there are sympathizers outside, they riot. In response to the large homemade flags glimpsed over the security walls the protesters press through the police lines towards the prison. By hand the two groups tear through several rings of fence and wall. Tearful refugees clench razor wire in bloody hands. The embraces of strangers—as they finally reach each other—are as powerful as any lovers. Fifty escape.

But we are in Goricko, the poorest, most geographically isolated region of Slovenia, which has become a major transit point for "illegal" immigrants, refugees and asylum seekers. The next morning we were meant to break camp but instead the majority of the noborder camp, some seventy strong, with anarchist flags unfurled, drums beating, lift the chain link fence and enter the compound. We dance, perform, and speak with those imprisoned inside. The action is videotaped, edited and distributed onward (www.dostje.org).

The presence of video in social movements keeps expanding as the costs for high quality digital video fall. The director of *This is What Democracy Looks Like* (www.bignoisefilms.com), one of the most widely screened activist documentaries to date, speaks of movement video surpassing mainstream media. During the WTO protests, CNN deployed two camera crews in Seattle, whereas *Democracy* drew on the footage of over 120 Indymedia video activists.

The explosion of video production is not simply the result of falling costs in camera and editing equipment, of course, but also of the multiplicity of uses that video can be put to as a tactical media. It is worth enumerating a few of them because they extend beyond the obvious, documenting movement activities.

As those who squatted Avtonomna Cona Molotov (www.acmolotov.org) in Ljubljana, Slovenia are quick to point out, sometimes only the visible presence of a camera constrains violence by the police and private security forces. Of course, sometimes, as was the case in Genoa, cameras are an inadequate deterrent and video becomes the record of police violence as well as evidence for lawsuits (italy.indymedia.org/news/2003/02/176245.php). Video can also play the role of fundraising material as is the case with the Antifasiticka Akcija Video CD (Antifascist Action, www.vjecniotpor.vze.com), the proceeds of which go toward the printing and distribution of the East European anarchist newsletter *Abolishing the Borders from Below.* The practical appeal of video activism speaks to the do-it-yourself dream of autonomous cultural production.

There is an irony. While the means of video production become more accessible, the most important means of distribution are corporately consolidated. Although some of the most developed movements prove that traditional broadcast technologies can be reappropriated—such as street television (www.telestreet.it) and satellite transmission (www.tvglobal.org)—the self-distributed CDs, VHS tapes, and poor quality streaming or downloadable video of most video activists do not fulfill the promise of a media revolution.

Yet video plays a more intangible role as a medium through which new senses of identity are imagined. Despite a frequent lack of formal creativity, not least a stylistic aping of mainstream news and music video, something more transformative has been set in motion. At a recent Subverzije (the Zagreb anarchist self-education sessions), a gathering of some fifty people watched a video about the crisis in Argentina. The path of this tape is itself telling. At the European Social Forum in Florence a Croatian activist purchased it from a touring French representative of the Zapatistas. The tape was carried on a bus of activists originating from Nis, Serbia, on their way to Croatia. In the video an unemployed physical laborer burns tires at a barricade on a highway near a refinery. He stares out of the screen and says: "I've heard about the protests in Seattle and Genoa against corporate globalization. I'm part of that struggle." Activists in a smoky socialist-era room in the Student Center stare back at him, nodding.

walking patient

Julia Meltzer

walking patient a patient whose injuries and/or illness are relatively minor, permitting the patient to walk and not require a litter

A nation of walking patients drive and walk and sometimes take the bus and are injured by our distance and complicity. Perhaps it is wrong to suggest that we are injured too? It's a different kind of wound, one that happens in reverse, from the inside out. On the surface, everything appears to be normal. One moment we're walking with confidence, and then suddenly a limb falls off without warning. Now we're limping and soon, crawling. An arm drops off and we use it for a crutch. Walking becomes impossible. A litter will soon be required.

we

Kathryn Chetkovich

We are all New Yorkers now.
Does that mean
starting today
that we agree to cast our lot
With the lot of them?
Not just with the Cambodian family
of five in one room
in Queens
but with the man downstairs
who beats his wife?
That we now see ourselves
in the young salesman smoking
on the corner and in the Muslim
cabbie who thinks homosexuality
is an abomination against God?
Even in the ones who seem,
for all the world,
just as rude and arrogant and
glad not to be us
as they were yesterday?
Are we really all one now?
I imagine God
(if speaking in words we could recognize),
would say Sort of.
But always and ever, not just *now*.
And *we* is a word that cleaves,
splitting even as it joins.
I and another, it says,
sometimes not including them
and sometimes
not including you.

weapons of mass destruction

Itty Abraham

As best as I can tell, the first detected use of weapons of mass destruction (WMD) is recorded in the Old Testament, a text revered by the Judeo-Christian-Islamic religions, when, in a fit of anger, Yahweh sends seven plagues to Egypt. Most of these weapons fall under present-day categories of biological and chemical weapons, some are indeterminate; together they wipe out a great deal of the kingdom's livestock, productive lands, and elite manpower. Hinduism too, not to be outdone by the other major religions, has its share of major weapon systems. Here the gods tend to appear as gatekeepers to the holy arsenal, providing warriors and sages with devastating weapons calibrated to the extent of their religious sacrifices. These tend to be single-issue weapons; however, their efficacy dissipated after their first, usually unplanned, use. Dare we then assume there may be a clash of civilizations implicit even in the memory of these weapons?

It would be easier to answer this question if we knew exactly what WMD are. The term itself is relatively new, a child of the fevered abstractions that swirled between Cambridge, Massachusetts, and Washington, D.C. in the 1950s. As time went on, WMD went out of semantic favor, resurfacing only in the aftermath of the Cold War and the rise of new threats to American military power. Now it seems, in a historically analogous moment of global anxiety, WMD are back. Every Eastern cult leader, tinpot dictator, shadowy Islamic terrorist and reformulated Communist may have one, be close to having one, or simply be thinking of having one, according to unnamed high official sources close to the Administration. Given the obvious bias in its everyday overuse, it is easy to dismiss WMD as just another loaded term-of-the-day, subject to the usual myopias of race, nation, and capital.

To take the term apart is to see its barriers to entry. The "Weapon" part of WMD can be a missile warhead loaded with toxic chemicals, a syringe full of killer anthrax, a petri dish of incurable viruses; but what is it not? Weapons are not the regular toxic spills from nuclear reactors, not the dumping of waste chemicals in local rivers, not tuberculosis bacteria that have become immune to repeated over-prescriptions of antibiotics, not the strange afflictions of environmental disease, mental illness, and other murky modern-day illnesses that escape the probe of medical instruments and electronic diagnostics, and certainly not the production of seeds that are programmed to commit suicide in a single harvest cycle. The "Mass" part refers to an undifferentiated people that translate into the body of the nation, a Western, powerful body that has a lot to lose, a homogenous group of ingénues who need to be protected at all costs from the above-mentioned threats. The "Mass" is never the millions who die from a lack of the most basic things for survival, the farmers who commit suicide because their debts have mounted beyond the ability to ever pay them back in this lifetime, the boy soldiers of countless wars of attrition taking place because of the wanton disregard for limits in the making of wealth, the young children who are trudged into seedy brothels in order to satisfy the demands of diseased sybarites. "Destruction" seems unambiguous, but, as we can see, selective.

Accident

What distinguishes the release of a cloud of toxic gas from a Union Carbide plant in Bhopal, killing thousands and crippling hundreds of thousands more, from Saddam Hussein's alleged use of poison gas against the Kurdish minority of Iraq? Both actions killed scores of people, but only one is typically classified as the use of WMD. Why? The answer, it appears, lies in the deliberateness of the act, the degree of awareness of the intended effects, the wantonness of the act of destruction. Hence, since Saddam Hussein's use of chemical weapons against the Kurds was done in the full awareness of what he was trying to achieve, i.e., their mass destruction, whereas Union Carbide's was not, the latter action falls into the category of an "industrial accident." The cause of the "accident" cannot be identified with any one actor, whether the designer of the plant, the employees, the owners or the state government of Madhya Pradesh. Calling the gas leak at Bhopal, and the thousands who died as a result, an "accident" makes the event akin to a natural disaster, a so-called act of God, not the use of a Weapon of Mass Destruction. Ultimately, this distinction is only possible because of a particular understanding of the nature of "accident." Is this distinction meaningful?

Large-scale complex modern technologies, whether oil refineries, steel mills, air traffic control systems, or chemical factories, are all built to a scale that makes them impossible to "know" completely. The omniscience we associate with the inventor of an artifact (the personal computer, for example) does not hold up when we consider these megatechnologies, both because no one person can master the complexity of the entire system, and second, because the system itself is greater than the sum of its modular parts. In other words, because of the scale and complexity of the system it is impossible to comprehend its totality. What can be known (or rather measured) is the output of certain key factors, inputs, variables, or products. If the measured value of these factors lies within certain bounds, then all is considered well. If not, there is a potential crisis.

In this context, an accident is an extreme kind of crisis, which can be expressed in terms of the extent to which key variables have exceeded acceptable limits. A crisis is usually measured in term of variables expressing its absence, usually "safety" or "efficiency." But what does a term like "99.9 percent efficiency" actually mean in practice? According to the popular U.S. magazine *Inc.*, in terms of (U.S.) standards, operating at a 99.9 percent level of perfection means the following: 16,000 pieces of mail lost by the U.S. Postal Service every hour, two unsafe landings a day at Chicago's O'Hare Airport, 500 incorrect surgical operations a week, 20,000 incorrect drug prescriptions a year, and 32,000 missed heartbeats a person annually. Few megatechnologies of the kind described above are nearly that reliable. "Accidents," in other words, are a structural feature of megatechnologies. Accidents cannot be done away with without getting rid of the technology. The distinction cannot hold.

Humanitarian intervention

One of popular culture's most vivid maxims is "Guns don't kill, people do," the seductively reasonable slogan of the U.S. National Rifle Association. The logic underlying this statement is familiar. Guns, whose only purpose is to kill living beings, are being discursively made into silent technical artifacts whose futures are determined by a single factor, the operator of the gun. Guns in the hands of the police and the patriotic citizen are good things; in the hands of the criminal or the terrorist are not. Likewise, the Weapon of Mass Destruction. What is critical is not the instrument or even its killing potential, but the mind of the person behind it. The ability to prevent weapons of mass destruction from proliferating across the globe then becomes the need to control those who might use these weapons for conscious purposes of mass destruction. We have shifted from the control of weapons to the control of those who might use them. The machine is made into a mute technical switch, a purely neutral object, and all attention must now be focused on the operator himself and his thought processes. The strategy of focusing attention on the man behind the machine allows for the full play of cultural difference to be read in racial and civilizational terms. He is now the "Rogue Leader" who must be stopped at all costs.

This is not new, but the contemporary logic of "intervention" in the making (and stopping) of Rogue Leaders is. The triangulation of three fronts for intervention—the transnational media, the international humanitarian industry, and political-military power—produces an endless stream of rogue states led by Rogue Leaders who can be found in Darkest Europe, sub-Saharan Africa, South Asia, North Korea, and the always popular Middle East. Weapons of mass destruction appear when the transnational media discovers a suitably recalcitrant and larger-than-life tyrant or rebel; the international humanitarian industry discovers the scores of victims that have been created by the actions of this tyrant or rebel, and finally, the military-intelligence complex discovers in the tyrant signs of interest in weapons of mass destruction, ideally funded through rents from their near-monopoly on some precious metal and mineral. If only one of these three fronts is present we get a momentary news event or a low-level humanitarian problem. If two are present, then the media joins the humanitarian industry and starts making a case for the importance of the event in relation to the well-being of "international society." If the conjuncture of politics is right, the military-intelligence forces step in and we have a full-fledged crisis, proclaimed on all three fronts. This was the Gulf War, East Timor, and Kosovo, but not Rwanda or Kashmir. Weapons of Mass Destruction are a product of the triangulation of interventionary fronts, not their cause.

we'll all be dead

Christopher Connery

> After the second interview with him on December 11, we got up and walked over to one of the doors. There are all of these doors in the Oval Office that lead outside. And he had his hands in his pocket, and I just asked, "Well, how is history likely to judge your Iraq war?"
>
> And he said, "History," and then he took his hands out of his pocket and kind of shrugged and extended his hands as if this is a way off. And then he said, "History, we don't know. We'll all be dead."
>
> —*Bob Woodward*[1]

That was a strange thing to say, in this death- and memorial-obsessed country, in this country that found its national sentiment, began its history really, over the graves of soldiers. Dead Ronald Reagan reminded us of the American way of death and history. The coffin that filled our screens day and night almost made up for the hidden coffins of Dover, Delaware, and a relieved though fantastic talk of History filled the airwaves again. What, then, to say about the Bush way of death? Through which of the Oval Office's many doors lies that secret?

He's not apocalyptically minded. The Christian code-words that fill his speeches have scant reference to Revelation or the end times. Ashcroft, maybe, but not W. The raptured, after all, might know something about time, history, and the descent into sin. He does, though, rail against what he calls the Death Tax, and that, I think, gives some insight into George W. Bush on life and death. He chooses death.

Marx understood the life-and-death struggle between capital and labor. The abolition of all rights of inheritance, third on the list of the *Communist Manifesto*'s ten-point transitional program, was one stake into the heart of the dead labor of an undying capital, which, "vampire-like, only lives by sucking living labor, and lives the more, the more labor it sucks."[2] Capital made George W. Bush, and his code of honor has committed his presidency to its necrolatrous regime. We'll all be dead. History won't matter. Dead labor will stalk the earth.

---

[1]Interview with Mike Wallace, *60 Minutes*, April 18, 2004.

[2]Karl Marx, *Capital*, Vol. 1, trans. Ben Fowkes (London: Penguin, 1976), 342.

wired

Bettina Stötzer

Words are important in wars. Sometimes refusals to speak the words of war make a difference. Sometimes we do better to garble speech rather than to speak clearly.

In 1914, a French telegraphist and a German civil servant—who never met each other—joined in an act of solidarity by letting the transmission of the German Declaration of War against France go haywire. They did not alter the text of a telegram sent by the German Chancellor's office to the German ambassador in Paris, but instead let the coding and decoding machines of the telegraph run loose. For a moment, the international technologies of secrecy failed all by themselves.

Upon its arrival in Paris, the message read, in part:

German expectations had brennerei kel Italian Ambassadors. We were respected border and advise July strictly to obey. On the other hand despite zone Elena with old mue erol and mountain road, agreement French together already regard mortgage physically 10 to you iu ge sen ante Howard ultramontan and in view of still in relatively area. . . . Communicate please crumbling field this afternoon 6 o'clock of there government, your passports demand and for delivery of the business to American Ambassador leave.[1]

If you can't understand the text, consider, neither could its receivers. For just a moment, nonsense won over the clarity of state aggression.

---

[1] Excerpt from text of the telegram, first published by the Dadaists in Zürich in 1918 and quoted at length in Alexander Kluge, *Chronik der Gefühle. Band II: Lebensläufe* (Frankfurt am Main: Suhrkamp, 2000), 993. The original is in German and this English translation is a product of a later kind of "translation machine" on the Internet (www.google.com/language_tools?hl = en).

words

Kasian Tejapira

Words move us through their music; the very sound of a word—its rhythm, its rhymes—moves us. Words can conjure people out on to the street to overthrow a government. Words can move people to fight, to die, to kill. But these are words that can be sung. This is why translation is so difficult; to be effective in their new context, translated words must recover their musicality. The Communist struggle in Thailand, which collapsed some twenty years ago, was perhaps the most sung and rhymed revolution in the world. Through recitation, words circulate and mobilize.

Consider this stanza from a poem, composed in the 1980s by Naowarat Pongpaiboon, winner of the SE Asia Write Award, to move us to consider the killing fields in Cambodia under the Khmer Rouge.

A million wrist-bones up-piling

ที่สูงส่งสูงสุดยิ่งจุดพลุ
ที่ต่ำใต้ไหม้ทะลุลงคาขื่อ
ฟ้าก็ร้อนดินก็ร้ายเร่งไฟฮือ
กระดูกมือล้านมือมารวมกอง

โดย เนาวรัตน์ พงษ์ไพบูลย์
กวีซีไรท์ ค.ศ. ๑๙๘๐
แต่งราวคริสต์ทศวรรษที่ ๑๙๘๐

Even as a non-Thai speaker, you can read the poem for its rhythms and rhymes.

Thi soong song soong sud ying jud phlu
Thi tam tai mai talu long kha kheu
Fa ko ron din ko rai reng fai heu
Kradook meu lan meu ma ruam kong

Here is the translation:

Those on top reach for the stars,
Those at the bottom fall down crashing.
Burning sky and barren land stoke up the flame,
A million wrist-bones up-piling.

In the process of translating and editing these words, Charoen Wataksorn, a friend of mine who is a popular community leader of a local grassroots movement to oppose a coal-powered electricity generator project in the south of Thailand, was shot dead on the night of June 21, 2004. I went there to attend his cremation over the weekend, and I was invited to give an impromptu speech in his memory. My daughter asked me why good people like my friend were so unfortunate in Thailand, why someone who fought, not in order to defeat anyone he hated, but to protect his home, got killed.

I did say something in answer to her heartbreaking questions, but it could never be good enough.

notes on contributors

Itty Abraham is the author of *The Making of the Indian Atomic Bomb* and various articles on science and security. He lives in New York.

Raymond Apthorpe is visiting fellow in international relations, Australian National University, and professorial research associate in social anthropology and development studies, London University.

Dalit Baum teaches women's studies in Israel and is an anti-occupation, social justice activist.

Amita Baviskar is at the University of California Berkeley, temporarily a legal alien on a J-1 visa.

Jonathan Beller is Associate Professor of English and Humanities at the Pratt Institute.

L. R. Berger's book *The Unexpected Aviary* received the 2003 Jane Kenyon Award for Outstanding Book of Poetry. She is an Associate of Pace e Bene, a nonviolence education service.

Iain Boal is associated with Retort, whose pamphlet *Afflicted Powers,* based on the broadside "Neither Their War Nor Their Peace," is forthcoming from Verso.

Margaret Brose is Professor of Literature at the University of California Santa Cruz. She writes on poetry and its transformative powers. Were it not for Dante's guidance, she would still be lost in Limbo.

Wendy Brown teaches political theory at the University of California Berkeley.

Sean Burns is a graduate student in the history of consciousness at the University of California Santa Cruz. His research focuses on the relationship between education and democracy in social justice struggles.

Wendy Call tries to find a happy medium between writing and editing, living in Gringolandia and Mexico, anarchism and Marxism, bioregionalism and global action.

Jeremy M. Campbell studies roads, natures, nativeness and modernity as a graduate student in cultural anthropology at the University of California Santa Cruz.

Ben Carson's great-grandmother was an ambulance driver in World War I. Now he engages various scientific and critical "theories of mind" to investigate musical consciousness.

Kathryn Chetkovich is the author of *Friendly Fire,* a collection of short stories. She lives in New York City and Boulder Creek, California.

Martha Collins has published four books of poems, including *Some Things Words Can Do.* She is Pauline Delaney Professor of Creative Writing at Oberlin College.

Christopher Connery teaches world literature and cultural studies at the University of California Santa Cruz.

Wendy Coxshall is a graduate student of social anthropology at the University of Manchester (U.K.). She loves chewing coca in the Andes and rejects violence.

Angela Y. Davis is Professor of History of Consciousness and Women's Studies at the University of California Santa Cruz. She has been engaged in (anti)prison activism for most of her life.

Mike Davis is a San Diego-based writer-activist and the author of *Dead Cities* and *Planet of Slums.* He has also published kids' science adventure novels.

Hilla Dayan is a Ph.D. student in sociology at the New School for Social Research, working on citizenship and surveillance in Israel/Palestine and apartheid South Africa.

Joseph Dumit is an Associate Professor of Anthropology and Science and Technology Studies at the Massachusetts Institute of Technology. He works on brains, drugs, facts, images, and social movements.

P. A. Ebron attended Belmont Elementary School in Philadelphia.

Bregje van Eekelen, a Ph.D. candidate at the University of California Santa Cruz, studies the social life of ideas.

Lieba Faier is a Mellon Postdoctoral Fellow at Cornell University. She spent twenty-three months conducting fieldwork in rural Nagano for her doctoral dissertation and is writing a book based on her experiences.

Kathy E. Ferguson is Professor of Political Science and Women's Studies at the University of Hawai'i. She and Phyllis Turnbull do research on global militarism.

Courtney L. Fitzpatrick is an artist and student of biology who watches lemurs in Duke Forest and runs polymerase chain reactions. She lives with her girlfriend, happily unmarried.

Jonathan Fox's most recent activist-scholar collaboration is *Indigenous Mexican Migrants in the United States* (www.ccis-ucsd.org/publications/indigenous.htm).

Carla Freccero is professor of Literature, Women's Studies, and History of Consciousness at the University of California Santa Cruz.

Carol Gluck teaches Japanese history at Columbia University.

Myra Goldberg used to write and teach fiction but now writes political pieces with pictures, teaches at Sarah Lawrence College, and tries to get her students to vote.

Jennifer González teaches at the Whitney Museum of American Art and the University of California Santa Cruz. Her forthcoming book addresses the intersection of race discourse and contemporary installation art.

Lisbeth Haas works at the Pentagon's Institute for Peace and Feminist Research that recently replaced the Departments of Homeland Security and Weaponry.

In 1953 **Donna Haraway** watched her dog-pound mutt, General Eisenhower, rescue her pet fowl, Chicken Little. Haraway now writes manifestos that link people with machines and animals in a search for livable worlds.

Sharon Hayes is an artist who uses multiple mediums—video, performance, sound—to investigate history, politics and speech in relation to processes of individual and collective subject formation.

Engseng Ho would like to know why Anglo-American power can't stop hectoring and lecturing. Some peace and quiet would be nice.

Karen Z. Ho is a cultural anthropologist who studies powerful communities in hopes of disarming them. She teaches at the University of Minnesota, Twin Cities.

Donna Hunter regularly teaches a course on the intertwining of death and patriotism at the University of California Santa Cruz.

Emily Jacir is an artist who lives and works between New York City and Ramallah, Palestine. Jacir was featured in the Istanbul Biennial of 2003, and the Whitney Biennial of 2004.

NeEddra James lives in the San Francisco Bay Area and is a Ph.D. student in the History of Consciousness Department at the University of California Santa Cruz.

Sushma Joshi is a freelance Renaissance activist/artist. She believes in political creativity, or creative politics, depending upon which medium she's using.

Afsaneh Kalantary is a Ph.D. candidate in cultural anthropology, an Azeri-Iranian-American, and a nomadic exile in the eternal waiting room of history.

S. Eben Kirksey has studied and is affiliated with the Organisasi Papua Merdeka (OPM), a movement that desires freedom for West Papua from Indonesia. In June 2004 John Ashcroft called the OPM a terrorist organization.

Morgen J. Lennox is an undergraduate student of anthropology at the University of California Santa Cruz. This work is dedicated to the memory of Alex B. Page.

Sven Lindqvist has published thirty books of essays, aphorisms, autobiography, documentary prose, travel and reportage. Internationally he is best known for his books on China, Latin America and Africa.

Lydia H. Liu teaches at the University of Michigan. Her favorite line of modern poetry is by the poet Bei Dao, who wrote: "Freedom is nothing but the distance between the hunter and the hunted."

Krista Geneviève Lynes is a doctoral candidate in the History of Consciousness Department at the University of California Santa Cruz.

Bahíyyih Maroon is a writer and queer mother who creates and renews just a little past dawn when the horizon is most tangibly bursting with tomorrow's possibilities.

Julia Meltzer is a media artist and director of Clockshop, a nonprofit media arts organization in Los Angeles. She is a 2004 Rockefeller Media Arts Fellow.

Helene Moglen holds a Presidential Chair in Literature at the University of California Santa Cruz, where she is also Director of the Institute for Advanced Feminist Research.

Goenawan Mohamad is an Indonesian writer living in Jakarta. He writes a weekly column in *Tempo,* the leading Indonesian weekly.

Annemarie Mol is a professor of political philosophy; she does multi-sited ethnographic fieldwork in order to write situated philosophy. She lives in the Netherlands.

Carole Simmons Oles is Professor of English and Creative Writing at California State University, Chico, and author of six books of poems.

Geeta Patel is Associate Professor of Women's Studies at Wellesley College. She has written on poetry, colonialism and politics, and is currently investigating the entanglements of desire with finance, risk, poetics and violence.

Mary Louise Pratt used to write squibs like these for *Tabloid: A Review of Mass Culture and Everyday Life,* produced by a collective at Stanford University in the early 1980s. She works at New York University now.

Vicente L. Rafael lives in Seattle and works on such topics as colonialism, nationalism and translation, especially with regard to the Philippines.

Lynn Randolph is a painter who lives and works in the conservative zone known as Houston, Texas. She does what she can to subvert the politics of good ol' boys and religious fanatics.

Maple Razsa is a social anthropologist, documentary filmmaker and activist. He is writing a dissertation on globalization from below among radical activists in the former Yugoslavia.

Adrienne Rich's latest poetry collection is *The School Among the Ruins.* She lives in Northern California.

Lisa Rofel teaches anthropology at the University of California Santa Cruz and has written about American Jewish responsibility towards peace and justice in the Middle East.

Renato Rosaldo has worked on a multicultural politics of the workplace. He has published a bilingual book of poems, *Prayer to Spider Woman / Rezo a la mujer araña.*

AnnJanette Rosga is Assistant Professor of Sociology at the University of Colorado at Boulder. Her research focuses on human rights and policing in emergent democracies.

New York–based artist **Martha Rosler** was awarded the Spectrum International Prize in Photography in 2003. Her essay book *Decoys and Disruptions* appeared in 2004.

James K. Rowe is a graduate student at the University of California Santa Cruz. He thinks (un)freedom comes in many forms, but prioritizes freedom as participation—and play.

Warren Sack is a software designer and media theorist. He teaches in the Film and Digital Media Department at the University of California Santa Cruz.

Larry Schwarm has been photographing prairie fires for fifteen years. His latest book is *On Fire.* He teaches at Emporia State University and is represented by San Francisco's Robert Koch Gallery.

James C. Scott teaches political science and anthropology and is Director of the Program of Agrarian Studies at Yale University.

At the great 1963 civil rights march, **Alix Kates Shulman** became a lifelong political activist. A feminist writer since 1967, her eleven books include four novels, two memoirs, and two books on the anarchist/feminist Emma Goldman.

Bettina Stötzer studies the history of racism and nationalism in Europe. She is a Ph.D. student at the University of California Santa Cruz, and holds an F-1 visa.

Marilyn Strathern's homes: wartime Manchester, London suburb, student Cambridge, Mbukl in highlands Papua New Guinea, Canberra & Port Moresby, and all over again (as professor, etc.) at Manchester, Cambridge and Girton College.

Neferti Tadiar is co-director of the Feminisms and Global War Project at the University of California Santa Cruz and author of *Fantasy-Production,* a treatise against contemporary nationalist fantasies of global power.

Kasian Tejapira was formerly a radical student activist and guerrilla fighter in the jungle of northeastern Thailand. He now teaches politics at Thammasat University and writes columns in various Thai newspapers.

David Thorne is an artist in Los Angeles. He is a 2004 recipient of a Rockefeller Media Arts Fellowship. Current projects include The Speculative Archive.

Jude Todd struggles to change her consuming habits and to avoid being consumed by the University of California Santa Cruz, where she teaches writing and interdisciplinary courses.

Anna Tsing has just published *Friction* to assess and nurture anti-imperial dialogue across city and countryside, north and south.

Phyllis Turnbull is a retired associate professor of political science at the University of Hawai'i who is trying, with reasonable luck, to reestablish indigenous plants and trees at her own homeland.

Yasushi Uchiyamada is Professor of Anthropology at the University of Tsukuba. He is among a group of citizens taking an action against the Japanese government for sending soldiers to Iraq against the constitution.

Neerja Vasishta is a tourist who just graduated from the Department of City and Regional Planning at Cornell University. She would like to visit Belize one day.

Kath Weston's latest book is *Gender in Real Time: Power and Transience in a Visual Age.* She is now writing on the rule of law and offshore incarceration.